*What people are saying about...*

# RISE UP

"Throughout the Bible we are told not to fear but trust in God's leading and yet fear continues to limit us and hold us back. I met Vanessa when she was a counselor at Camp Glisson and have watched her ministry blossom and mature brilliantly for almost twenty years. Vanessa Myers offers up a warm, honest, and refreshing peek into her own journey of facing fears and learning to lean on the promises of God. Walk with her page by page as she shares the fears she carried and learn each scriptural road sign she discovered that helped lead her forward in faith."

**Rev. Micheal Selleck,** retired pastor and former Director of Connectional Ministries of the North Georgia Conference of the United Methodist Church

"As a children's ministry colleague of Vanessa's, I am more than happy to recommend her book, *Rise Up*. Vanessa writes personally, honestly and effectively about the fears faced in ministry, and then uses scripture to offer ways to overcome them. All who serve in ministry will be able to relate to this book and benefit from it."

**Glenys Nellist,** author of the children's book series, *Love Letters from God*, Children's Ministry Coordinator of the West Michigan Conference of the United Methodist Church

"I am grateful for the opportunity that I have had to serve in ministry alongside of Vanessa Myers. It was apparent in that time that she had a tremendous heart and calling for children and families. In her first book *Rise Up*, she articulates what we have all felt at one time or another. Her stories, illustrations, and use of Scripture help everyone who wants to be a servant face and confront their own fears. Vanessa turns the mirror on herself to give her readers the confidence and courage to step out faithfully in their own ministry settings."

**Rev./Dr. Jeff Ross,** retired pastor of the North Georgia Conference of the United Methodist Church

"If you have ever faced FEAR in ministry, and who hasn't, this book is for you. Vanessa delves into the realities of the fears we face and how you can break free from those fears and find the freedom to not only do the ministry God has called you to do but learn to enjoy it along the way. This book will give you the tools to rise higher and realize that every time you face obstacles, God has already equipped you to overcome them. Get this book and watch God move you past your fears and into your destiny."

**Craig Johnson,** Director of Ministries at Lakewood Church in Houston, TX, author of *Champion* and *Lead Vertically*

"We have all been there. We've been paralyzed in fear at the thought that God wants to use us in ministry. That is why I am thankful for Vanessa's new book, *Rise Up*. She shares her journey with a transparent lens that not only captures you but challenges and convicts you to evaluate your fears as they correlate with your call to ministry. I am also grateful for her real life examples as well as her constant use of scripture as her source for truth and encouragement. *Rise Up* will be a great resource for one new in the ministry as well as the seasoned servant."

**Danielle Bell,** Minister to Children, Dawson Church in Birmingham, AL

"A vulnerable, strong leader is hard to find... especially one who shares their heart as powerfully and with as much eloquence as Vanessa Myers. That's why I'm so thankful for leaders like her who will take the risk to share their journey with others in order to be used by God as a catalyst for healing.

In her new book *Rise Up*, Vanessa offers practical strategies out of her own journey that will help anyone serving in ministry rise up and fulfill the divine calling on their life with strength and purpose. As a ministry leader for seventeen years and one who works specifically in the area of helping creatives overcome roadblocks to their calling, it's my pleasure to highly recommend this book to anyone who's ready to rise up and go to their next level in God!"

**Matt Tommey,** artist, speaker, and author of *Unlocking the Heart of the Artist*

# RISE UP

*Choosing Faith over Fear
in Christian Ministry*

**VANESSA MYERS**

**EQUIP PRESS**
*Colorado Springs, Colorado*

# RISE UP

*Choosing Faith over Fear*
*in Christian Ministry*

Published by Equip Press, Colorado Springs, Colorado.

Unless otherwise designated, scripture quotations contained herein are taken from (NRSV) the New Revised Standard Version Bible, copyright © 1989 the Division of Christian Education of the National Council of the Churches of Christ in the United States of America. Used by permission. All rights reserved.

Scripture quotations marked (NIV) are taken from the Holy Bible, New International Version. Copyright © 1973, 1978, 1984, 2011 by Biblica, Inc.® Used by permission. All rights reserved worldwide.

Scripture quotations marked (NLT) are taken from the Holy Bible, New Living Translation, copyright © 1996, 2004, 2015 by Tyndale House Foundation. Used by permission of Tyndale House Publishers, Inc., Carol Stream, Illinois 60188. All rights reserved.

Scripture quotations marked (CEB) are taken from the Common English Bible ™ copyright © 2010, 2011 by Common English Bible. Used by permission. All rights reserved.

First Edition: 2018
Rise Up: Choosing Faith over Fear in Christian Ministry / Vanessa Myers
Paperback ISBN: 978-1-946453-27-3
eBook ISBN: 978-1-946453-28-0

*For my mother*
*Thank you for being my cheerleader, my supporter,*
*my encourager, and for teaching me about Jesus.*

# Contents

# ACKNOWLEDGMENTS

I first and foremost want to thank God for calling me to write. I never would have imagined that God would use me to write a book about the fear of serving Him. Thank you, Lord, for giving me the courage to share my story. I pray it will encourage someone else.

A special thanks to my husband, Andrew, for supporting me throughout the writing of this book. And to my children, Rae Lynn, and Shelby for giving me grace when I was writing.

Thank you to my small group friends and my Thursday morning Bible study ladies for supporting me through this journey and encouraging me to go after my dream.

Thank you to Kathryn Watson, my developmental editor, who helped me tremendously with this book. I truly appreciate your guidance in my writing.

And a big thanks to Michele Tennesen and everyone at Equip Press for guiding me through the publishing process and helping my dream become a reality.

# INTRODUCTION

In that moment, all I wanted to do was quit.

I was the center of attention in a room full of people. All eyes were on me during the yearly evaluation at my church. I listened, helplessly, as my peers and employers critiqued the job I was doing.

*You're good at that, but you need to work on this.*

*Don't do that again.*

*We don't like it when you do this. Can you do more of this instead?*

The list of comments grew and grew. I know there had to be some positive ones, but the negatives echoed in my head.

What I was really hearing was: *You're not good enough. We don't like you. You stink.*

I remember coming home and collapsing into my husband's arms, sobbing, and telling him that I didn't want to go back to work. Ministry was not supposed to be like this. If I had been truly called by God, I shouldn't have to endure hurtful words. I am trying my best so why is it not good enough for some people?

*If this is what ministry is going to be like, then I want out.*

Seventeen years have passed since I first began working in the ministry. Though my self-doubt and insecurities have evolved as a fruit of my experience, it would be dishonest of me to pretend like I have stopped feeling the same fear and dread of criticism. At times, fear in particular has consumed my thoughts. It has even prevented me from stepping out in faith when God has called me to act.

I felt like Paul did in 2 Corinthians 11:28 when he said: "And besides other things, I am under daily pressure because of my anxiety for all the churches."

When I first read this passage, I screamed out, "Yes, Lord!" This is how I feel.

I want the job I do for the Lord to be perfect. I want everyone to like me. I want everyone to think I do a good job. I want it to be easy without any roadblocks or hurdles that I have to jump over. I want to have lots of friends and be happy all the time. I want ministry life to be fun and carefree, not laced with the fears that have crippled me over the past seventeen years.

Ministry life hasn't been and won't be perfect for me or for you. It won't be free from hardships. God doesn't call us to serve Him because it's easy. In fact, He never promises that it will be. He just asks us to come and follow Him.

In 2 Corinthians 12, Paul writes to the church at Corinth about speaking the truth about Jesus and being grateful for the trials he has had to endure. He even says,

"So I will boast all the more gladly of my weaknesses, so that the power of Christ may dwell in me" (verse 9).

Who wants to boast about their weaknesses? Who even likes to admit they are weak? I know I don't. The fears I have experienced have weakened me. They have made me feel that I can't do anything.

When I felt God calling me to write this book and to share my experience of fear with you, I absolutely did not want to do it. Fear is my weakness. I don't want to openly talk about it. I don't even want others to know about it. What if sharing my story just leads people to question why God is even using me?

But, here is what I have learned over the past few years: I am not alone in my fears. I have encountered others who have the same fears of serving the Lord.

I once led a workshop called, "Being a Woman in the Ministry". This session focused on how women seem to build a wall of fear that prevents them from serving God faithfully. In this session, we built a wall of our fears using paper bricks. The women wrote down their fears on the bricks and we hung them on the wall. I was amazed to see this huge wall of fears. It was then that I realized I am not alone in this fearing God thing. And it was my confirmation that I needed to write this book about the fear I have had as a woman in the ministry. I need to show others how God has brought me out of the darkness of fear into the light of His provision and calling.

You don't have to be afraid of doing what God has called you to do because Jesus is right there with you. I want you to cry out to God and ask Him to rise up against the enemy who has held you hostage to fear and hasn't allowed you to break free. I want you to take the hand of Jesus and let Him lead you out into the light.

A Bible verse that has spoken greatly to me as I have faced my fears of serving God comes from Jeremiah 17:7-8 (NIV):

"But blessed is the one who trusts in the Lord, whose confidence is in him. They will be like a tree planted by the water that sends out its roots by the stream. It does not fear when heat comes; its leaves are always green. It has no worries in a year of drought and never fails to bear fruit."

I want to be that tree. I want my roots deeply planted in God so that when I serve Him, the fear that the devil throws at me will not bring me down. I want to stand strong on God's promises and be victorious over fear. I want to be free from fear so that I can bear fruit for the Lord.

And that's what I want each of you to feel, too. I want you to boldly step out and serve God. And that means letting go of the fear that keeps you hidden in the dark. I want you to rise up and see the freedom that God gives you from fear.

# 1

# THE BIG FEAR
## *Fear of God's Calling*

*O*f course he wanted to serve God, but he was not doing *that. That was crazy!*

Jonah was a prophet, but this was asking too much from him. How could God expect him to do something as crazy as tell the Ninevites that they needed to repent and turn from their wicked ways? They didn't deserve to be saved. They deserved the punishment that was coming to them from God.

He had to get away from the Lord. God's presence right in that moment was too much. If he could flee from the Lord then all would be good and he would feel better. He didn't like what God was calling him to do.

And so he ran.

Jonah found a boat setting sail for the city of Tarshish and climbed aboard with the confidence of knowing he had escaped from the presence of the Lord. He was safe. No more voices calling him to do crazy things.

But then the boat began tossing about in the storm. With each crash of the wave against the ship, the men aboard grew fearful. They needed to get rid of a few things to lighten their load. Maybe that would allow their ship to stay afloat in this powerful storm.

Nothing seemed to work, though.

If it wasn't the cargo, then the problem must be that man that just came aboard. He's got to be running from something.

So the crew threw Jonah off. As soon as he was off the boat, the storm ceased.

But God didn't leave Jonah alone.

He sent a large fish to swallow him. For three days, he sat in the belly of that fish. And that's when Jonah changed his mind and decided he needed to go and do what God had called him to do.

### My Calling

Have you ever heard that voice? You know…the still, small voice of God? Even though we can't audibly hear God's voice, we know when God is speaking to us. We know when God is calling us to do something. It's a feeling you have and you just know that it's God's voice.

I remember the day I first heard His voice clearly. It was a hot summer day in Georgia in the summer of 1996. I was working at Camp Glisson, a United Methodist Church Camp in the North Georgia mountains. I grew up going to this camp as a child, and was now fulfilling my dream as a camp counselor.

I had taken my group of high school girls to the Dining Hall Porch to do an activity. This stone porch provided the much needed break from the scorching summer sun. As we were sitting there, the other counselor in our group began leading the activity. As I was listening to her, my mind drifted to this other voice I heard:

*"Come, Vanessa. Serve me in the ministry."*

What? Who was that? Was someone speaking to me? I looked around, but didn't see anyone else except the girls in our group. None of them were looking at me, either. They were paying attention to the other counselor as she spoke. It had to be God. It was strange, but at the same time very comforting. God wanted me to do something for Him.

Then I got this feeling. I can't explain it, but it was just this very real sense of the Holy Spirit. I felt the presence of the Lord and it was amazing. That's when I knew the Lord was calling me into the ministry.

### Time to Run

Just because I heard God's voice calling me doesn't mean I listened. I didn't need God to tell me what to be when I grew up. I already had it figured out. I wasn't going to change my plans to fit His. So, I laced up my shoes and ran in the opposite direction.

Since my junior year in high school I wanted to be a physical therapist, after one of my good friends was in a car wreck. She was paralyzed from the waist down. She was in a rehab center for many months because she had broken her neck and had many other injuries. She needed help every day from the doctors and therapists so that she could learn to function without the use of her legs. I would go to the rehab center every now and then and watch as the physical therapists worked with her, doing exercises to help her muscles gain control. She gained back her upper body strength, but her legs would not work. She was paralyzed, and was told she would be for the rest of her life.

As I watched the physical therapists, I realized that I wanted to become one. I wanted to help people. I researched schools that offered physical therapy and decided on North Georgia College (which is now called the University of North Georgia). North Georgia had a great physical therapy school. I decided my major was going to be Biology/Pre-Physical Therapy. I was ready and excited to pursue this degree.

When I started my junior year, I had to take Genetics. That was the hardest class ever! My brain couldn't wrap itself around the concept of genes and how it all worked. I decided to drop that class, which meant I could no longer be a Biology major. But, that didn't mean I couldn't still be Pre-Physical Therapy. I could get a Psychology degree and also be Pre-Physical Therapy. I still heard God's voice speaking to me, but I kept running, hoping He would change His mind. I wasn't ready to give up my dream of being a physical therapist just yet.

As time went on, I worked hard in my studies. I worked even harder as it came time to apply for graduate school. For two years I tried getting into a Physical Therapy graduate school program. I would get interviews, but was never selected.

It hurt.

Why couldn't I get into at least one of the schools? Was I not good enough? Talk about having your dreams shattered. It was so hard to think that what I wanted to do for the rest of my life wasn't going to happen.

During those two years of trying to get into Physical Therapy school, God kept speaking to me about going into the ministry. He's really good at making sure you hear Him. I've learned that He likes to give you the same message in many different ways.

One significant moment I remember actually happened at the church I am on staff at now. When I was in college at North Georgia I would occasionally attend Dahlonega United Methodist Church. The only Sunday I went in January of 1997, the pastor spoke about being called by God. He told us not to forget to do the thing that God has called us to do. Don't ignore God and turn your back on Him or run away from Him. Do what He has called you to do.

I listened in amazement. The one Sunday I come to this church and this was the message? Not a coincidence; it was all God. There was that voice again. I heard it. I felt it. Was I going to stop running away or was I going to listen?

Well, being a twenty-year-old at that time, I decided I would keep running the other way…for now.

Since I had changed my major in the beginning of my junior year of college, I was behind a year. I had to go five years to finish my Bachelor's degree. As I came into my last semester at North Georgia, I began to panic. What was I going to do with a college degree in Psychology? What kind of job would I be able to get? I applied to three different graduate schools in three different fields: social work, speech pathology, and seminary. I figured maybe I would get accepted into one of these, and then I would know for sure that was the field I was supposed to enter.

God had to be laughing right about now. I can just hear Him saying, *"Vanessa, why are you doing everything but listening? Why not just listen so things would be easier?"*

I needed 100% confirmation the voice I was hearing was God. I needed one more sign the voice was from Him.

Well, God gave it to me. Of the three graduate programs I applied to, the only one that accepted me was Duke Divinity School.

At this point, I stopped running.

There was that voice speaking to me, loud and clear. *"Go to seminary. This is where I want you. This is the path that I have chosen for you so you can serve Me."*

When I stopped running, I felt relief. I know that sounds crazy, but I think I was just happy not to be running anymore. Believe me, I was tired of running. It's exhausting trying to do your own thing and having it not work out. I was ready to be obedient. I was ready to stop being afraid of God and what He was calling me to do.

### Why Are We Afraid?

God's calling can be very scary. We don't always know what's going to happen. We can't map out how things will turn out. We can't see the future clearly. And because we don't know what's going to happen, we run the other way, the opposite way that God is leading.

There are many different reasons why we might run from God's calling. One reason is the fear that this calling might not be from God. What if this calling is of our own desire? Maybe it's a dream you have but are afraid to take a risk because you fear doing what God really wants you to do.

I can say for sure I have had these thoughts many times. This has happened more so in the last three years. God has placed a new calling in my life. That calling is to write and speak. I have questioned God, constantly asking Him if this is what He wants me to do, especially when I felt called to write this book. I want this book to succeed. But what I want most is to glorify the name of God. I want this book to give God the glory for all that He has done in my life when it comes to fear.

When I think about writing, I question whether I heard God right. Maybe it's my own selfish desire to write a book and have it published. Maybe I'm the one putting this passion and love of writing into my own heart. Maybe

I really want to succeed and give myself the glory. How can I know for sure?

All I can tell you is that God has confirmed this calling over and over to me. The first main confirmation from God is that He took my hatred of writing and turned it into a love. That can only be from God. Also, when I write articles or post on my blog, I am encouraged by my readers. And then there's another kind of confirmation you get when you are browsing the internet and you see a banner on your computer screen in big bold letters, "Has God called you to write? Then do it." God knows that sometimes we need to see things in writing and using the computer screen (where I am at a lot of the time), is a great way to get my attention. When the question is already in your heart and God has already been speaking to you about it... this kind of confirmation is just icing on the cake. And you may be the only one who knows it, but you know that it is confirmation from the Lord.

God knows we need multiple confirmations that the calling is from Him. He knows we are only human and need special guidance. He wants us to know it's Him speaking. One of the ways you can know that it is Him, is when you hear the same message coming from multiple sources. Everywhere we turn we are hearing His voice: in Scripture, in the words of another person, in music, in a devotional, or maybe even on a huge billboard on the side of the interstate or a banner on your computer screen. God will confirm your calling in several different ways so you will know without a shadow of a doubt that this calling is from Him.

Another reason we can be afraid of God's calling is the fear of having to depend on Him for provision. With accepting the call from God we will have to take risks and some of those risks involve finances, friends, jobs, home, and our comfort zone. And with those risks come a lot of questions: Will I have enough money to provide for my family? Will I be able to buy things I want? How will I pay for my bills? If I move, will I be able to make new friends? Will my kids be able to make new friends? Will they like their new schools? Will I even like the new job or new calling for my life? Where will I live?

When it comes to provision, we tend to shy away from God. We feel that it's up to us to provide for ourselves. If God calls us to do something, we analyze that calling, and try to figure out for ourselves if we can manage it. My husband does a lot of this when I tell him about something I feel God is calling me to do. He'll run the numbers, make a spreadsheet, and come back with an answer to whether we can financially do that or not. But in the end, he always rips those spreadsheets up and realizes he can't figure it out. He has learned that the only thing he and I both can do is to trust God.

When I think about the provision of the Lord, I am reminded of one of the names of God: "Jehovah-Jireh". It's the Hebrew word that means "The Lord will provide." You can find this referenced in the book of Genesis 22. Abraham has gone up the mountain as the Lord had asked him to sacrifice his son, Isaac. Thinking they were going to be sacrificing a lamb, Isaac kept asking his father where the lamb was. I can only imagine the heartache Abraham was experiencing as he tied up his son and was preparing to sacrifice him. He was probably wondering if God really was going to make him do this.

Abraham was a man of faith and obedience. He followed God's calling even when he wasn't sure how God would provide. He just trusted and knew that God would give him all he needed. And God did provide for Abraham on that mountain. A ram appeared ready for the sacrifice. Because of his obedience a whole nation was descended from him.

This story of Abraham and Isaac is a foreshadowing of what God provided for every one of us. A perfect lamb. One without blemish. Sacrificed for us. He took on the sins of the whole world and died so that we could live eternally.

If God is willing to provide His own son to take on all our sins, why are we so afraid that He won't provide for us when He calls us? Why can't we trust in Him completely?

Fear can make us feel, think, and act in some pretty crazy ways, especially when it comes to obeying the call from the Lord. But we have to remain focused on His call. We must remember His promises and how He will always be with us. We must remember those Ebenezer moments in our lives.

### Ebenezer Moment

In the book of 1 Samuel 7:5-13, Samuel assembles all of Israel at Mizpah and tells them to fast and confess their sins before God. When the Philistines heard the Israelites were near, they got ready to attack them. The Israelites became afraid, but Samuel tells them:

> "Do not stop crying out to the Lord our God for us, that he may rescue us from the hand of the Philistines" (1 Samuel 7:8, NIV).

Samuel took a lamb and offered it to the Lord as a sacrifice. During this time, the Philistines came to attack, but the Lord interceded for the Israelites. When they came out to attack, the Philistines were defeated. After this it says:

> "Then Samuel took a stone and set it up between Mizpah and Shen. He named it Ebenezer, saying, 'Thus far the Lord has helped us'" (1 Samuel 7:12, NIV).

This stone was a remembrance for the Israelites. Samuel wanted them to never forget how the Lord provided for them against the Philistines. He wanted them to remember this defining moment in their lives.

God's calling for me to serve Him in the ministry was a defining moment in my life: an Ebenezer moment. God had been preparing me all of my life for that moment when I heard His calling at Camp Glisson. He had been helping me for nineteen years to hear Him speak to me in that spot.

Why do I feel that way?

Because God used someone else to help me get to Camp Glisson. I had been a camper there since fourth grade and attended every year (except one) up until twelfth grade. The spring before my first summer there, my parents separated and eventually divorced. My mom wasn't working at the time and we had no money. Yes, my father paid child support, but it wasn't enough to cover the extra things we wanted to do, like go to church camp. However, someone in my church paid my way to go to camp that summer. I have no idea who it was, but their generosity and kindness paved the road for a greater calling in my life.

The summer of 1996 was a moment that God had ordained. He used the events of my life before that to prepare me. It was an Ebenezer moment because I could see that "Thus far the Lord has helped me" (1 Samuel 7:12b).

### Finding Freedom

I had hit the giant wall of the fear of God's calling. It was blocking me, not allowing me to see over it or go around it. All I could do was turn around and run the other way. But I was tired of running. I wanted to listen and follow Him, but I needed to find a way to knock this wall of fear down.

I don't know about you, but I don't want to be afraid of God's calling. I want to be brave and press forward through the fear. I don't want the fear to stop me. But what can I do when faced with this fear?

I love that God's plan for helping me find freedom for each of these fears can be found in Scripture. If you are ready to conquer that great big fear of His calling, you need to take a look at our good friend, Paul, a man who had a burning desire to tell others about Jesus. What he writes in Romans 12:11-12 is exactly the tool we need to knock down that wall of fear between us and God.

Before we dive into Romans, I think the very first step we need to do to overcome this fear is to remember the day we were saved. I like to call it my "I belong to God" day. This is the day when you make the biggest decision of your life. It's a major turning point in everyone's life. You realize that you belong to God and want nothing more than to do everything you can to serve Him.

So, why should we remember our salvation day?

Because it's a major day in our lives; another Ebenezer moment for sure. And it helps to remember it because it puts your calling into perspective.

Think about it.

If you hadn't given your life to Jesus, would you be receiving this call from God? Who knows what your life would be like at this moment if you didn't have Jesus? But you do. And you can look back at that day of salvation and be grateful that you made the decision to follow Christ.

I remember my salvation day because I did one thing to help me never forget it…I wrote down the date in my Bible. It was October 23, 1988. I was twelve years old. I remember sitting in my room at home and praying and asking Jesus into my heart. No one else was around. It was just me and the Lord. I also remember thinking that I didn't ever want to forget that day so I wrote it down in my Bible. I am so grateful that I did.

Both of my daughters have accepted Jesus and have written down their salvation days in their Bibles, too. I also teach the kids in my church to do the same thing. I want them to never forget the importance of that day.

I don't read from that copy of the Bible any more, but I still have it on my shelf. Any time I get afraid of something God calls me to do, I get it out and I look at that date. It helps me to remember the importance of that decision. If I could make the decision to follow Christ for the rest of my life, then I could step up and do the things He wants me to do. There is no reason to be afraid of God's plan for my life. No reason at all.

Let's jump back and take a look at the awesome disciple named Paul. Talk about a man on fire for the Lord. His desire for Jesus burned so brightly in him that he just had to get it out and talk about Jesus. In Romans 12:11-12, Paul is speaking to the Romans about what it means to be a new Christian. What he lists here is a perfect plan for helping you overcome your fear of God's calling. Here is what that passage in Romans says:

> "Don't hesitate to be enthusiastic – be on fire in the Spirit as you serve the Lord! Be happy in your hope, stand your ground when you're in trouble, and devote yourselves to prayer" (Romans 12:11-12, CEB).

Let's take a closer look at these four points of action:

First, we must be enthusiastic and on fire! Now, I'm not saying you have to go out and be all peppy and start yelling. But, I can tell you that when you have that fire for the Lord, you'll want to shout it out everywhere you go. You won't be able to hold it in. It has to get out. You must share Jesus with others. It will show in your words and in your actions. The love and desire to share Him will be overflowing.

Note here, though, that you can't fake enthusiasm. You can't pretend to be excited and on fire. You may be terrified on the inside, but on the outside, if you try to fake your excitement then people will see right through you. You can tell when people are faking things, right? I think you'll be able to tell when someone isn't being sincere and honest about their love for Jesus. True and pure enthusiasm for Jesus will be contagious. It will catch on quick and others will want to share in that same passion you have for our Lord and Savior.

The second step in overcoming the fear of God's calling is to be happy in your hope. Other translations say to "rejoice in hope" (NRSV). So how do we be happy about hope and what does that have to do with God's calling in your life?

When we accepted Jesus as our Savior, we became believers in the hope that He provides. A hope that He is with us. A hope that He will take care of us. A hope that He will provide for us. A hope that He has a plan for our life. A hope that He is all-knowing. A hope that His love will never fail. That's what we believe when we accept the love Christ offers to us. And who wouldn't be happy in that hope?

When we become afraid of God's calling, we have, in essence, become afraid of the hope that goes along with believing in Christ. We have forgotten all those reasons why we believe and hope in Jesus. The fear of His calling blocks us from remembering the hope we have. So, when we become afraid, we need to remember our hope and be happy. We need to rejoice and be confident in Christ. There is no reason to fear that great big calling from Him, especially when we know that Jesus never fails. The next time you are afraid, be happy in your hope in the Lord. Do a little happy dance if you need to. I think if you do, it will put a huge smile on your face as you rejoice in hope in the one true God.

The third step in overcoming your fear of His calling is to stand your ground when in trouble. Other translations say "be patient in suffering" (NRSV). This is an extremely hard step; one not many people find easy. Who wants to suffer? Nobody, that's who. So, why should we be patient in suffering when it comes to letting go of the fear of God's calling?

Consider this step to be your reality check. We all need these sometimes. Life is not fair and things are going to happen that hurt us. But, sometimes we seem to lose that sense of reality when God calls on us. Maybe we get this misconception that because God calls us then we will be free from anything that can harm us. That is the furthest thing from the truth. God never promises an easy road. What God does promise, though, is that He will never leave us.

Suffering will come in our lifetime and I'm pretty sure you will experience that suffering when you are doing the thing God calls you to do. Believe me, I've endured it myself.

But what does Paul remind us to do? He says we need to be patient in our suffering. And we know that's so hard to do. When tragedy strikes, when we are sick, when we are criticized, when we feel alone, or when we feel far from the Lord, we must be patient in our suffering. We must stand our ground and keep going.

The last step we need to take in order to overcome the fear of God's calling is to devote ourselves to prayer. Paul talks a lot about prayer throughout the Bible and not just in this verse in Romans 12.

In 1 Thessalonians 5:17, Paul says we need to "pray without ceasing" (NRSV). In Colossians 4:2 Paul says, "Devote yourselves to prayer, keeping alert in it with an attitude of thanksgiving" (NRSV). In Ephesians 6:18 Paul says, "Pray in the Spirit at all times and on every occasion. Stay alert and be persistent in your prayers for all believers everywhere" (NLT). And in 1 Timothy 2:1, Paul says, "First of all, then, I urge that supplications, prayers, intercessions, and thanksgivings be made for everyone" (NRSV).

Paul didn't take prayer lightly. He believed wholeheartedly in the power of prayer. He believed that prayer changes lives. He had seen firsthand the difference when people pray.

When we are afraid to do what God has called us to do, we must commit to being devoted in prayer. It's at this point where we need to be down on our knees talking non-stop to our Lord. This is the time where our prayer life should be on fire. Don't we want to know exactly what God is calling us to? Don't we want to be obedient to whatever it is God wants?

The answer to all these questions is yes. However, fear blocks us from God. And fear comes from the enemy. The devil does not want us to know what God wants us to do. What do we typically do when we meet fear face to face? We run the other way. We don't pray and we try to get as far away from God as we can.

But prayer is our key to keeping us in close communion with God. Devoting ourselves to prayer, like Paul suggests, is what will help us stay focused on God's calling. It's what will help us maintain an excitement about being used by God. Prayer will knock down that wall of apprehension that separates us from believing that God will sustain us. It will help us serve God without fear of His calling and be ready to do whatever it is He asks of us.

### Don't Let Fear Win

God's calling for us can be terrifying at times. What I don't want you to do, though, is get to a point where you let fear win. That's when we turn away from God and don't let Him use us for what He created us for. We can't let fear win!

I have had to knock down this wall of fear. A lot. And I'm sure I will have to kick it over more times over the course of my life. I now know how I can conquer it. I wish I had known these things when I was nineteen years old. Maybe then I wouldn't have had to face such hardships in my years of serving in the ministry.

All the fears I have faced in the seventeen years of being in the ministry have helped shape who I am today. I am an overcomer. And you are called to be one, too.

### Rise Up Prayer

*Almighty Father, You created us for a purpose. You have given us skills and talents to help us serve You for that purpose. Each of my friends reading this hear Your calling, but fear of doing what You have called them to do prohibits them from living for You and for the purpose that You created them for. We cry out to You today, Lord, and ask You to rise up against the enemy who is throwing us off course by allowing us to believe the lies he puts into our hearts. Give us the strength to stand up and press forward, doing what we know You have called us to do. Help us to have faith in You like we have never had before so that we can boldly serve You in what You ask of us. In Jesus' name we pray, Amen.*

## 2

# WHAT'S AN EXEGESIS?
### *Fear of Learning More*

There it sits. A beautifully wrapped box, covered in gold and adorned with the finest of jewels. It's a box fit for a king. And not just any king. But the King of Kings. The Lord of Lords. The One and only true God.

This is your God Box.

Inside this delicate and magnificent box is where we store all of our knowledge of God. This box holds all the information we have learned throughout our life about Him. Each time we learn something new, we add it to our God box.

It's full of stories from the Bible we learned in Sunday school as kids, as well as Scripture verses that we hold near and dear to us; ones that we memorized so that we could recall them at a moment's notice. It's full of God's promises and His love for us, as well as forgiveness that He gives so freely to us through the death of Jesus Christ, so that we in turn can forgive others. It's full of memories of how God has provided for us, as well as memories of those who have been Jesus to us. It's a full box.

The box is full to the point that it is packed, and we think we have learned all we can about God and who He is. How can we possibly learn anything new? The box can't fit any more knowledge.

So we close it.

### *Learning More: Round One*

I remember the day perfectly. I went to the post office at my college and inside my mail box was a big manila envelope from Duke Divinity School. Everyone knows that big envelopes mean good things. I ripped into the envelope and found the words I was hoping to see: *"Congratulations! You have been accepted into the Masters of Church Ministries program at Duke Divinity School."* I was so excited! I ran out of the post office, down the hill, and was ready to share the good news with someone I knew.

The excitement of being accepted into seminary soon faded, and fear set in. What was there to fear when I had just been accepted into a school where I would further my knowledge of God and the Bible? I had fears of a new place and new people to meet, but mostly a fear that I would not be smart enough to learn so much about the Lord. This was a great opportunity for me and I needed to get rid of this fear. But my feet seemed to be perfectly planted in the ground, unwilling to move.

One reason I didn't want to go was because I thought I had learned everything possible there was to know about God. I was raised in a Christian home where we went to church every Sunday. I was a faithful member of my church, attending worship and Sunday school. I had memorized Scripture when I was a kid (thanks to those M&M's from my teacher that motivated me). I worked at a church camp where I could talk about God all the time to others. I read my Bible (maybe not every day, but I did read it). I had filled my God Box to where I didn't think anything else could fit in.

I convinced myself I didn't need to learn anymore about God because there was nothing else to learn.

But then one day I had lunch with my college campus minister, and the advice she gave me turned my thoughts around. She said that, yes, I could go into the ministry without having gone to seminary, but to really think about all I could learn from being there and how I would greatly benefit from the classes. After our conversation I concluded that I did need to go to seminary. I needed that next level of training and understanding of the Bible, Christian education, and theology. I would be a better leader for it.

Stepping foot on Duke's campus was amazing. I couldn't believe I was a student at Duke University. Entering the halls of the Divinity School was a new world for me: new people, new professors who knew a lot more than I did, books I had never heard of before, a library that held many books and resources about the Bible, and a majestic chapel where I was able to attend services like no other I had experienced. So many new things.

After sitting through a few days of classes, another fear of learning more emerged. I began feeling that I was not smart enough to learn more about God. I wasn't really prepared for entering a theological school. I had been to church my whole life, but yet I did not understand everything my professors were saying. What were these words they were using? I had no clue what they meant. I felt stupid, like I didn't even know the Bible. How could that be? I had been reading the stories from the Bible since I was a child. Why did I not understand the terminology and concepts being taught in theology school?

I began to question even more why – or even if – God had called me here to learn more.

And then God showed me why in Hebrews 5:12-14:

"For though by this time you ought to be teachers, you need someone to teach you again the basic elements of the oracles of God. You need milk, not solid food; for everyone who lives on milk, being still an infant, is unskilled in the word of righteousness. But solid food is for the mature, for those whose faculties have been trained by practice to distinguish good from evil."

There it was, in plain daylight. Because I was being called by God to lead others and teach them about the Bible, I needed advanced training.

The teaching I had received growing up was wonderful. It taught me about God, Jesus, and all the many amazing stories from the Bible. My parents, grandparents, church, and friends had taught me so much and it was the best foundation I could receive.

But when I was called by God to serve Him in the ministry, I was called to a higher level. I needed deeper training in His Word. I needed to learn more so I could teach others more about Him. I needed to receive solid food.

Some of you reading this may be saying, "Well, I'm called by God to lead others in the ministry, but I don't think I need advanced training." Maybe not. But I do believe that in order for us to serve God fully, we must seek to know more about Him. For me at that time, that included going to seminary to receive my Master's degree.

### *Learning More: Round Two*

Life in the ministry is focused on others and helping them grow in their relationship with the Lord. At times, you may forget to invest in your own relationship with God. You can forget about what you need to learn about God each and every day and to seek Him first.

Being a Children's Minister, I don't often get to go to worship. I am always doing my job with the kids while others attend worship services. It can take a toll on your soul if you are the one constantly teaching and giving and don't take time to deepen your relationship with God and learn more about Him.

That realization hit home about four years ago for me. I had this strong desire to read my Bible and do Bible studies. I craved the Word of the Lord and wanted to know more. I was spending time with God each day, but I wasn't really learning much because my heart was not all the way in. I realized that I was afraid. I was afraid of this strong desire to seek the Lord because I was afraid of what God would tell me. I believe there are many people out there who crave more of the Lord but are too afraid to spend time with Him because they fear what God might reveal to them about themselves, about what He wants them to do, or about what they will learn from the Lord. We are comfortable with where we are spiritually and don't feel we need to seek the Lord. Our God Box is extremely full. What else can God tell us that He already hasn't told us?

God wants to speak to us, but the first thing we need to do is dive into the sea of the Lord. This means diving into everything that can teach us more about Him. That includes reading the Bible, doing Bible studies and learning about God from others.

One of my favorite organizations is Proverbs 31 Ministries. This is a ministry for women that provides encouragement and helps you learn more about the Lord. Proverbs 31 Ministries offers an app called First Five. They created this app because they wanted to help teach others the importance of giving God the first five minutes of each day. They take a book of the Bible and study it. Each day is a different chapter of the book. Their timeline is to be able to go through all sixty-six books of the Bible in four years.

When I first started doing this, I wasn't reading the chapter of the Bible along with the app. I was just reading the devotion on the app. But God, once again, laid it on my heart that to really learn more about Him, I needed to read His Word. I am happy to say that today I read each chapter of the book of the Bible we are studying, write down the verses I feel God is showing me that day, and also read the devotion on the app. And I am amazed as my eyes are opened to learning more about God.

The Bible is the same as it's always been. It hasn't changed from when I was a child. None of the books have different meanings. It's all the same.

But I have found that even though I have read the whole Bible cover to cover, I am learning something new each time I open it. Every time I read the Bible I make sure to read it slowly, digesting every word and letting them soak in. I find this is helpful and allows God to show me things I might have once been too afraid to see. And this practice takes patience as I am a person who wants to do everything fast. Sitting still and slowly reading is hard for me, but my patience pays off as I learn more about my Lord.

Another learning opportunity with Proverbs 31 Ministries is their Online Bible Studies (OBS). I knew this would be perfect for me since I was not always able to take time during the day to attend studies at our church. I fell in love with Proverbs 31 OBS and began to read every book they studied. Each book has opened my God Box more and more to let new knowledge of God in.

I also believe that part of our seeking the Lord is learning more about Him from others. After having done online Bible studies for a few months, I realized I needed real life people to learn from. I needed the community that only a small group could provide. So I gathered eight women together and we began our own Bible Study. We meet at the local Starbucks once a week in the early morning and we discuss the Bible study books we are reading or we tackle a book of the Bible. It has been an amazing time of learning more about the Lord from His body.

The connection to God is breath-taking when we dive into His Word, do more Bible studies, and learn more from others. It will change your life and open up your heart to allow God to move in and through you. You will act differently and speak differently. And some people might just call you that crazy woman who loves the Lord.

### *Learning More = Craziness*

In the book of Acts, we see Paul make a huge transformation from persecuting Christians to boldly speaking the Word of God to the Gentiles. During this time, he learned from God and from others (the disciples). He was taught and he went on to preach the name of Jesus to those who had never heard of Him. He faced hardship and persecution himself, especially from the Jews. He was put in prison several times. But he never stopped speaking, and he never stopped learning from God.

In chapter twenty-six of Acts, Paul is in prison and has been there for about two years or more. None of the leadership feels like he should be in prison because he has done nothing to warrant death or imprisonment. The leaders (Claudius Lysias, Felix, Festus, and King Agrippa) don't want to upset the Jews, so they keep Paul in prison.

Every time Paul is brought before one of these leaders he is given a chance to speak his case. And each time Paul sees this as an opportunity to speak about Jesus. His mission is to help everyone believe in Jesus and change their ways. There comes a time when Paul is speaking before Festus and King Agrippa in Acts chapter twenty-six. Festus calls Paul crazy!

> "While he was making this defense, Festus exclaimed, 'You are out of your mind, Paul! Too much learning is driving you insane!'" (Acts 26:24).

When I first read that, I laughed out loud. How funny to see that a leader in the government called Paul crazy because of all the learning from the Lord! I am sure there are people you know that have called you crazy because of the things you speak boldly about Jesus. Some people cannot comprehend why we would want to learn about Jesus and why we would ever speak about Him to others.

Friends, I urge you to keep learning, even if people turn their backs on you or call you crazy. Don't give up. God wants to reveal Himself more and more to you.

### *Finding Freedom*

Is God calling you to learn more about Him? Are you afraid to do that because of what He might say to you? Will learning more take you into a deeper relationship with Him? Should you ignore this calling from God to learn more?

It's tempting to let this fear of learning more about Him take over your heart. That way you don't have to worry about growing closer to Him. You can just keep God at a distance and maybe He'll leave you alone.

Well, we all know that God's desire is not to leave us alone. He desires a closer relationship with each of us. And the way we get a deeper, more personal relationship with Him is by learning more about Him.

If you find yourself faced with this fear of really learning more about God, you need to do the total opposite of what you think you want to do. Instead of running from God and refusing to learn more, you need to seek God with all you have. But how does one go about seeking God?

For me, seeking God involves the 3 F's: fasting, feeding, and falling silent.

I once listened to a sermon series by Louie Giglio called "Habit."[1] In one of his sermons from this series called "The Piñata and the Iceberg", Louie talked about how he wanted this year for us to be a year of seeking the Lord. And that requires good spiritual disciplines or habits. It means that we need to have a deep relationship with Jesus so we can hear the Lord speaking to us.

---

1   www.passioncitychurch.com

Louie challenged listeners to do a twenty-one day fast. This should be a fast from whatever is keeping us from hearing from God and having that deep relationship with Him. Anything we are doing more of than listening to the Lord is a distraction and not a good habit.

During the long process of writing this book, I got to a point where I needed to fast. Not from writing, but from what was keeping me from writing. For me, that was social media and television. I can sit on Facebook or Instagram all day reading the posts and knowing everything going on in my friend's lives. Right now, I am tempted to pick up my phone to quickly check to see if I have any updates on my social media accounts.

And then there's television. We decided to save money and cut out our satellite TV bill and instead subscribe to Netflix. I love Netflix, but it is a time sucker. I can sit in front of the TV all afternoon binge-watching my favorite shows. Next thing I know, it's dark and time for bed. Where did my afternoon go?

I decided I needed to take Louie's advice, and for the next twenty-one days I fasted from social media and television. I won't lie. It was very hard, especially when your family sits in the living room and watches it. All I wanted to do was sit in there with them. It took everything I had in me to turn the other way.

During those twenty-one days, I began seeking the Lord. Which leads me into the second F of our action plan: feeding. No, I'm not talking about feeding yourself with food and eating till your stomach hurts. I am talking about feeding on the Word of God. Feasting on every word. I love what Deuteronomy 8:3 says:

> "He humbled you by letting you hunger, then by feeding you with manna, with which neither you nor your ancestors were acquainted, in order to make you understand that one does not live by bread alone, but by every word that comes from the mouth of the Lord."

I was feeding my soul with the wrong thing. I was allowing social media and television to feed me. I was soaking in every word from those two things and letting it take over my soul. I had forgotten to feed on the Word of God.

During my fast, I opened my Bible, wrote in my journal, read devotions, and read books. When I didn't understand something or wanted to learn more about a word I had read in God's Word, I researched it. I found out the meaning behind it and how it applied to my life. I allowed my soul to feast on every word from God. And friends...it was fabulous.

I found God speaking to me at every corner during this special time. And I learned so much about our ultimate Creator. He revealed Himself to me and I loved it.

After feeding on the Word of the Lord, I had to do another thing that was hard for me: fall silent. Silence is uncomfortable. Ever been in a room with someone you don't know and expected to make conversation? After a few minutes of shooting the breeze, you run out of things to talk about. And then there's the silence…and it's awkward.

I have always had a hard time being silent because I don't like the awkwardness. I feel like I have to fill that space with something. When I fall silent before the Lord I have really had to un-learn the need to fill space. I have had to learn to sit and be still. And that's when I can feel Him close. That's when I can get a glimpse of our Father. That's when I can hear Him speaking.

During those twenty-one days, God spoke and I learned. He is my Teacher and He revealed Himself to me. It's amazing what will happen when we take the time to seek the Lord.

Don't let your fear of learning more about Him take over. There is nothing to fear when it comes to being near to God. His love is overwhelming. His words are soothing. His presence is life changing.

Whatever God is calling you to, don't be afraid of seeking Him to know more about Him. His calling for your life is important, but His desire for you to know Him trumps all.

Open your God Box. Fill it. And then keep the learning continuously flowing. Your box has no bottom to it. No matter your age, your God Box will always need filling. Keeping it open will allow you to remember to continually seek the Lord.

### Rise Up Prayer

*Creator God, we thank You for giving us a desire to learn more about You. Rise up against the enemy, the one who longs to prevent us from seeking You; the one who would love nothing more than for us to turn away from learning more about You. Renew our passion and desire to seek You. Give each of my friends a heart on fire for opening up Your Word and digging in to find You alive on every page. Thank You for seeking us and may we in turn seek You in all that we do. In Jesus' name, Amen.*

## 3

# IS ANYONE THERE?
## *Fear of Loneliness*

It was an easy place to hide. The cave was dark and went back far. If he hid in the corners of it, then no one would find him. He especially didn't want to be found by the ones seeking his life.

David was the future king of Israel. But, he didn't much feel like a king. What king has to run for his life and hide in a dark, smelly, cold cave? But, he had to hide. Saul was looking to kill him. But only because Saul was jealous of David. He didn't like that David was strong, powerful in battle, and had killed tens of thousands more than him. Saul wanted David destroyed so he could reign forever.

David had a lot of time to think and pray while in that dark cave. No one was around and even though he was physically alone, he knew those feelings of loneliness were not just from being without the presence of people.

Ever since he was anointed as the next king of Israel, he experienced loneliness in a whole new way.

God had appointed him and set him apart from others. He was called by God to lead the nation of Israel; a task that was special, but one he knew would not be easy. But for some reason, this new calling for his life set him apart in a way he did not like. People started hating him. Some were jealous of him, especially King Saul. A man he admired and looked up to suddenly hated him and wanted him dead. All because he was chosen by God to be the next king.

Even though he was surrounded by others, the loneliness he felt was overwhelming. How could he feel this way when he saw people every day? But the loneliness he felt wasn't just because he was without the support and love from others. He felt abandoned by God.

God had called him to be the next king of Israel. He didn't ask God to make him king. God chose him. Why did he feel like God had forgotten about him? Wasn't God supposed to be with him all the time, leading him to be the best king Israel has ever had?

David hadn't even taken the throne yet and already the loneliness he felt was beyond anything he had felt before. All he wanted was to go back to before God had called him, to a time when he was just a shepherd tending his sheep. At least then he felt loved by others and no one was jealous of him or trying to take his life. Life before God's calling seemed peaceful and free from troubles. Why did God call him to serve as the next king, only to abandon him and make him feel so alone?

He cried out to God many times during this dark and lonely time. He needed to feel God's presence and he needed to feel God's love.

"Turn to me and be gracious to me, for I am lonely and afflicted. Relieve the troubles of my heart, and bring me out of my distress" (Psalm 25:16-17).

### My Loneliness Without People

My first experience with loneliness in the ministry came in the job I took right out of seminary.

I entered my last semester at Duke Divinity and realized it was time to start looking for a job in the ministry. My focus was in Christian Education. I had experience working with teenagers during my years at Camp Glisson so I began to look for jobs in Youth Ministry. A different job came to me, though, thanks to a friend. It was at a church camp in North Carolina and with my experience and love for camping ministry, I applied there.

I was offered the job as the new Faith Formation and Retreat Ministries Coordinator. I was excited about this new opportunity and ready to work at another United Methodist Church Camp. I loved being a camp counselor, so this would be a fun job...or so I thought.

I quickly learned full-time camping ministry was not the same as being a camp counselor. This was a "real" job, with huge responsibilities. I worked a lot. And I mean *a lot*.

The summer was fun as I got to work with campers, but after summer camp ended, my work really picked up.

I was at the office all the time, especially on the weekends when retreat groups were at camp. My job was to make sure they had everything they needed. That meant staying Friday night, all day Saturday, and Sunday until lunch.

During those long weekends, the loneliness started to kick in. How can you be lonely at a camp when so many people are there all the time?

Believe me, you can be lonely.

I had no friends (well, I did have one friend who worked at the camp with me, but she was just as busy). I couldn't go out on the weekends, but even if I could, there was nowhere to go. This camp was in the middle of nowhere. Literally. Nothing there. I'm not even sure where I went to buy groceries. That's how small this town was.

My friends were three hours away. My family lived many, many miles away in Georgia. For someone who never gets homesick…I was homesick. I wanted the people I loved to be close to me. I just needed to get rid of this loneliness feeling because I was not used to it.

Another thing that made the loneliness grow was the fact that I was not able to go to church on Sundays. Because my job required me to attend to the retreat groups at camp, I had to be there at every meal and especially when the groups packed up to go home on Sundays. That meant I could not go to church. Taking that out of my weekly habits was very hard. I missed worshiping God in that setting. I missed the friendships the church brings. I missed the Bible studies. I missed connecting with children and teens in that setting. I missed the body of Christ.

Was this season of loneliness a part of God's calling for me?

Maybe.

One thing I do know for sure is that during that year of isolation, God was there. He never left me nor abandoned me. I cried out to Him and He delivered me.

After about eight months, I couldn't take the loneliness anymore. I was ready for a new job. I needed people. And so the search for a new job began.

God took me to a wonderful church that accepted me and loved me. I had people in my life. And that felt good.

### *Loneliness Surrounded By People*

For anyone who serves in the ministry, I think I can safely say you have, at some point, experienced loneliness in your calling even though you are surrounded by many people.

The loneliness in my calling comes and goes. At times I have felt loved and surrounded by others who love Jesus as much as I do. The churches I have served in have been welcoming, supportive, and I have made some wonderful friends.

At other times, I have felt isolated. Sometimes that isolation came from a lack of support from the church in my job. I felt like no one was for me and all were against me. That's a hard part of ministry, too. If you are like me, you want everyone to like you. But, the reality is, not everyone will. Look at David. Not everyone liked him. It's a part of the calling. One that's often difficult to accept.

There's also the isolation you feel when, because of your calling into ministry, you are put on a pedestal and held to a higher standard. That means people around you think you are holy and they can't socialize with you outside the walls of ministry life.

I once had someone tell me they thought I was the holiest person they'd ever known. And while that was an amazing compliment, it was also hard to hear. I don't want to be seen as "holier than thou". I don't want to be seen as someone who can't be approached or as someone you can't socialize with. I want to have friends and I want others to see me as another human being; one who is a sinner and messes up. I laugh at times when others ask me if it's okay if they drink a beer. Or when they let a bad word slip, they apologize and ask forgiveness from me. I'm not sitting up on my pedestal looking down on others. That's not my job.

I'm not holy. I'm just a servant of God who loves God and tries hard to live by His Word. I mess up and make mistakes, just like anybody else.

I don't like the loneliness that comes with serving the Lord. It's difficult. But to be in the ministry requires the willingness to follow God wherever He leads. That may mean you serve Him abroad, leaving behind a world that has been your safe zone. Or it could mean you serve right where you are.

No matter where you serve the Lord, I am sure at some point you will experience a loneliness where you crave the presence of people. And I believe your reactions to the loneliness will be much like David's.

## *Loneliness Reactions*

One of the first things we do when faced with loneliness is question our calling. Did we hear God right? Are we sure we are doing what He wants us to do? Why would God call us to serve Him only to experience a loneliness that hurts?

And then, just like David, we question God and His presence in our life. David was not afraid to cry out to God in his loneliness and affliction. In Psalm 13:1 he says, "How long, O Lord? Will you forget me forever? How long will you hide your face from me?" And in Psalm 10:1 David cries, "Why, O Lord, do you stand far off? Why do you hide yourself in times of trouble?"

When we experience loneliness, we so desperately want to feel God's presence. When we look throughout the Psalms, we see a man who not only questions God, but one who drops to his knees and begins praying. And so we follow the example of David, and are driven to our knees and pray. All we desire is to feel the closeness that the Lord promises us. We long to feel the companionship that God provides each day. We truly want to feel the peace He gives when He is with us.

I love how throughout the Psalms, David, after he cries out or questions God, turns these around and praises the Lord.

"But I trust in your unfailing love; my heart rejoices in your salvation. I will sing the Lord's praise, for he has been good to me" (Psalm 13:5-6, NIV).

"The Lord is king forever and ever; the nations will perish from his land. You, Lord, hear the desire of the afflicted; you encourage them, and you listen to their cry" (Psalm 10:16-17, NIV).

"I will give thanks to the Lord because of his righteousness; I will sing the praises of the name of the Lord Most High" (Psalm 7:17, NIV).

David provides a good example for us. Yes, it's okay to question God or cry out to Him. I believe God actually wants us to do these things. But we must remember to praise the Lord through those dark, lonely times. And finding freedom from loneliness comes when we can remember God and press into Him.

### *Finding Freedom*

The Word of God is full of promises from Him. All we have to do is open it up and begin reading. The main promise we need to stand on when dealing with loneliness is to remember that God promises we are not alone. We can see that from the following Scriptures:

"It is the Lord who goes before you. He will be with you; he will not fail you or forsake you. Do not fear or be dismayed" (Deuteronomy 31:8).

"No one shall be able to stand against you all the days of your life. As I was with Moses, so I will be with you; I will not fail you or forsake you" (Joshua 1:5).

"Even though I walk through the darkest valley, I fear no evil; for you are with me; your rod and your staff – they comfort me" (Psalm 23:4).

"Do not fear, for I am with you, do not be afraid, for I am your God" (Isaiah 41:10).

What powerful words for all of us to hear. God's Word is the same today as it was back then. He will never leave us. When you are fearful or lonely, just get out your Bible and turn to Scripture. All throughout the Bible, we see how God is present, even in the lonely times.

The second step we need to take to get us through our fear of loneliness is to press into the Lord. Pressing into the Lord, I believe, involves a few steps: being aware of His presence, reading the Bible, and singing.

We must tune in to God. That means being aware of His presence. Before you get out of bed, talk with God. Don't check your phone to see what's happening on Facebook or read your emails. Don't begin thinking about your to-do list for the day. Don't even get up to take a shower. Just lie there and speak with God. Say, *"Good morning, God!"* Thank Him for another day to serve Him. And then be silent and let Him speak to you. When you are aware of His presence first thing in the morning, you are more likely to see Him during the day.

Every single day you need to look for God's fingerprints on your life. Where was God? How did you see God? Where did He leave a mark on your life today? Be aware of Him. Know He is there.

Next, you need to spend time in His Word. Get out your Bible. Read it. Soak it up. When you read the Bible, you feel God. You know you are not alone. You know He is present with you. The loneliness will decrease and God's presence will increase.

Lastly, we need to sing. Yes, I said sing. Even if you aren't any good. Just sing your heart out to God. Praise Him. Lift your hands. Glorify His name.

One of the things I love to do is sing. Now, I may not be any good at it (although I don't think I'm horrible), but ask my kids and my husband and they will tell you that I sing a lot around the house (and quite loudly, too). But my favorite time to sing is when I am by myself. I like to put in my earbuds, plug them into my phone and sing my heart out to God. I will do this at home or sometimes I even go into the sanctuary at our church in the early morning when no one is there yet. I sing and sing loudly. So anyone that comes and knocks on my door at home or happens to enter the church may hear me singing. But I don't care. I am not singing for others. I am singing for God.

For me, when I sing I can truly feel God's presence. When I sing, I am praising Him and glorifying His name and that in turn allows me to feel Him. Do you ever get those goose bumps or chills when you are singing to God? I do. That is when I can feel His presence.

Ministry work is lonely, whether you are out in the middle of nowhere or surrounded by many people. The loneliness you will feel in ministry will always make an appearance while you are serving God. But God has helped me overcome loneliness. He has given me the assurance I am not alone. He has given me a way to work through those lonely times should they ever rise again. And they will rise again. But now I can face that loneliness with a different perspective. I can remember the example of David, rest in His promises, and press into Him.

God is there. Can you feel His presence?

### Rise Up Prayer

*Ever Present God, You know that loneliness is very much alive here in our world and among Your people. Thank You for the promises You provide us with in Scripture that affirm Your presence with us here on the earth. We ask for You to rise up, O Lord. Take away the enemy of loneliness, the one whose desire is for us to feel like You are not present with us. Help us to stand on Your promises and be filled with Your Spirit of truth. May we boldly serve You, never fearing loneliness, but always aware of Your presence with us. In Jesus' name, Amen.*

# 4

# ANXIETY RISES
## *Fear of Change*

*He could feel his heart beating faster and faster. Oxygen seemed to be diminishing as he couldn't catch his breath. Panic started to set in. But why? He was in great health. Nothing physically wrong with him. Why did he feel like he might die?*

And then it hit Moses…his life was about to change significantly. Moses, the shepherd who lived in Midian, just had a conversation with God. And from all places, a burning bush (which was a little crazy in itself). God told him He saw His people being oppressed in Egypt and He was going to deliver them. He wanted to use him to be the leader and help rescue the Israelites from slavery.

That must be the reason why he felt this way. Things were getting ready to change big-time for him. No longer would he be a shepherd in Midian. God was going to use him to deliver the Israelites out of Egypt, where they were slaves, and bring them to the Promised Land. Not a small task, either. God had just told him that he would be a leader of many people. He was going to have to speak to the powerful Pharaoh and get him to release his slaves. He was going to have to take charge of hundreds of thousands of people and lead them.

Moses knew it was impossible, but at first he held out hope that God had spoken to the wrong person. Surely there was somebody else out there who could do a better job than he could. God obviously didn't know him very well. He tried to talk his way out of it. Who was he to talk to Pharaoh? And didn't God know that he couldn't speak very well? He was not eloquent with words. He was super slow when he did speak. No one would listen to someone like him. He would get laughed out of the room.

But God didn't seem to be listening to him. For every excuse he gave, God gave an answer, a way He would help him. God seemed to have this figured out. All Moses had to do was obey and follow Him.

The more he thought about it, the more panic he seemed to feel. The room started spinning, his heart felt like it might beat out of his chest, the air flow into his lungs seemed to be less and less, and his chest hurt. He really did think he was going to die. Why did God want to use him? Why did God choose him to be the leader? Why did God want to change his life?

***Anxiety Sets In***

I said goodbye to the loneliness the camp job brought and said hello to a church job as a Youth Director. Life was so much better. It was a great church, filled with many extraordinary teenagers and families, a caring and loving staff, and friends close by. I dove all in to my new job. *This was it.* This was what had been missing in my life. I loved church and I was so happy to finally be in it again.

After about seven months there, I began dating someone new. His name was Andrew and he was someone I had grown up with. Andrew and my older sister, Luanne, had been good friends since elementary school. Actually, her husband, Chris, and Andrew were best friends. I had known Andrew pretty much my whole life and now we were actually dating. About a month into dating, I knew he was the one. We were going to get married one day. He felt the same way.

So, here I was: great job, awesome boyfriend, and a beautiful city to live in. Everything was going well. Until that night I woke up and couldn't breathe.

I sat straight up in my bed. Why was it so hard to take deep breaths? I couldn't get enough oxygen. My brain was in panic mode. *I need to get out of here. I need fresh air.* I opened the door that led out to the porch of my apartment and gasped for air. My thoughts were not good ones. *I am dying. I am going to die right here on this porch and nobody will ever know it.* I cried out to God. *Please save me!*

It seemed to last for an eternity. Finally, I felt normal again. My chest stopped hurting and I was able to breathe regularly. What in the world just happened? Why did I feel that way? What came over me? I had been asleep and resting well, but suddenly woke up not able to breathe.

Days went by and it happened again. But this time it was in the middle of the day. I tried not to freak out in front of my co-workers. I wanted to remain calm. It took all I had not to scream and cry. This was not fun. I decided I needed to see a doctor. Something could be wrong with my heart.

Thoughts of death consumed me. I was worried and afraid. I didn't want to die. I was happy with my life. I was only 26 years old. I wasn't overweight or unhealthy. So, why could I not breathe?

Over the course of several months I went through many tests: X-rays, blood tests, echocardiograms, stress tests. You name it...I think I had it done. Throughout all this time, the doctor kept prescribing anti-depressants (which did not work at all because they made me feel like I was going to jump out of my skin). The one pill that did work was Xanax. I took only half a pill of the smallest dose and it seemed to calm me down whenever I felt that feeling coming on. Even though the pill helped calm me, no one could really say what was wrong with me.

During my echocardiogram, the cardiologist actually said: "Why are you here? You have the healthiest heart of anyone!" Well, I don't know why, except for the fact that my heart hurts and I can't breathe! Something was wrong. Why couldn't anyone find a physical problem with me?

After the doctor had completed months of testing, he finally asked me: "What is going on in your life?" Well, let's see…I got engaged, we decided to live in Georgia so I have to move, which means I have to leave a job I love, I have to find a new job in Georgia, I have to plan a wedding, we need to sell Andrew's house, and we need to buy a new house. Only just a few things going on.

The doctor finally hit the nail on the head. "Good news…you aren't dying. However, you are having anxiety attacks." Anxiety? I didn't feel worried about anything. But, he said, when so many things are changing in your life at one time, your body can react in a way that is not normal to you.

2003 became my year of anxiety. Even after the diagnosis and Xanax prescription (which did help), I still kept having attacks. *When will I get better? Will this ever go away?* I prayed a lot and kept those attacks to myself. I felt like a freak and a failure. How could I let things get so out of control that it caused me to feel like I was dying?

If you have ever had an anxiety or panic attack before, then you know how scary it can be. You know how real it is, too. The one time I did go to the hospital for it, the doctor made me feel stupid when he told me there wasn't anything wrong with me. He told me to go home and rest. Well, gee, if it was that easy, then I wouldn't have been in the hospital!

Changes were happening all around me. Good changes, like getting married. I was so happy and ready to be married to Andrew. I was excited to move back to Georgia. I would be very close to my family. I had missed them over the past few years while I lived in North Carolina. But, there were also some scary changes ahead, too: leaving behind a church I absolutely loved, job searching, interviewing, and trying to find the place where God wanted to use me. Those were all changes I was afraid of. Even though I loved Andrew and wanted to move back to Georgia, I was truly afraid of having to find another job because I was so in love with the one I had.

For someone who was looking forward to all the changes in her life, my body sure was not reacting well to them. I was super excited, but I was also very nervous. Unsure of the unknown, lots to do, and just flat out feeling scared.

### Did Moses Have Anxiety?

As I reflect back on all these changes that happened to me, I am reminded of the story of Moses. He had many changes in his life. Right from the start he was sent away in a basket down the river. He was raised by Pharaoh's daughter, and he had to flee to Midian after he killed an Egyptian - lots of crazy changes. And then one day as he is out keeping the flock of his father-in-law, Jethro, he comes across a burning bush. This is it. This is the defining moment that would change the course of his life forever.

Moses was afraid. The Bible doesn't come out specifically and say, "Moses was afraid" (except in Exodus 3:6 when it says he was afraid to look at God in the burning bush). But, no one makes excuses for themselves and tries to get out of doing something if they aren't afraid. I wonder if Moses had any anxiety attacks back in his tent, away from everyone? I wonder if he ever felt like he couldn't breathe, like he was about to die? I wonder if he ever got so nervous that he threw up? I wonder if he ever cried because he was afraid? Did Moses have any of these feelings?

Change was abounding in Moses. God was calling him to something greater...to a monumental task that scared him. First he had to convince a powerful man like Pharaoh to "let my people go" (Exodus 5:1). That definitely would not be a simple task. Pharaoh's heart was hard and it took ten plagues to convince him that God is the one true God and He is more powerful. I wonder if Moses ever got anxious or worried every time a plague came? The Bible doesn't mention until the fourth plague that the Israelites were safe from these bad things happening. Moses and Aaron were safe from all of them, but I am sure there had to be fear in seeing God bring about these horrible events. Why wouldn't Pharaoh listen? *Please, just let my people go so God does not bring about more horrible plagues for the Egyptians.* Finally, Pharaoh did and the Israelites were free.

Another circumstance Moses had to deal with was the anger of the Israelites. Moses was not very well liked, even from the beginning. In Exodus 5, Moses first goes to Pharaoh and asks him to release the Israelites. Pharaoh says no way and then decides the Israelites need more work. No longer could the Egyptians give them the straw to make the bricks. They had to go and collect the straw themselves and make the same amount of straw in the same amount of time. More work for the Israelites and they were mad. They said to Moses: "The Lord look upon you and judge! You have brought us into bad odor with Pharaoh and his officials, and have put a sword in their hand to kill us" (Exodus 5:21). I don't know about Moses, but if I had many people mad at me like that, then I think I would flee to find a safe place to hide.

The Israelites' anger didn't stop there either. We all know they were extremely upset with Moses and God for leading them into the wilderness, for having them only eat manna and quail every day, and then basically going around in circles for forty years. Steaming mad were these Israelites. No wonder it took them forty years to get to the Promised Land. These people were never satisfied.

Change after change after change occurred in the life of Moses because he was called by God. Same thing happened with me (and probably you). Both Moses and I were excited that God was going to use us to do many great things for Him. Of all the people in the world, God called Moses and God called me. However, we both feared the change that was about to take place in our lives. Moses tried talking his way out of it. Me? I just decided I would worry and stress about it, which caused my body to have anxiety attacks.

### Finding Freedom

I remember the day I was over it. I didn't like this anxiety and I wanted it gone. But I was confused because I had no idea how to rid myself of it. I felt so out of control and not sure how to stop something I didn't know how to stop.

God spoke to me and He helped me see Him. I was finally able to see through to the other side. Before, I had just relied on myself and what I could see…which wasn't anything but a dark cloud of stress, worry, and anxiety. However, God opened my eyes to see His path. I just had to walk with God and take each step with Him.

Those steps were revealed to me through one Scripture…Philippians 4:4-7:

"Rejoice in the Lord always; again I will say, Rejoice. Let your gentleness be known to everyone. The Lord is near. Do not worry about anything, but in everything by prayer and supplication with thanksgiving let your requests be made known to God. And the peace of God which surpasses all understanding, will guard your hearts and your minds in Christ Jesus."

Merriam-Webster Dictionary defines rejoice as: "to feel or show that you are very happy about something."[2] So, to rejoice in the Lord, as this passage in Philippians says, we must show that we are very happy in the Lord. And the best way for me to show this is to sing! Singing can do wonders to your soul.

---

2   "rejoice." Merriam-Webster Dictionary; Merriam-Webster.com. 2016. http://www.merriam-webster.com (June 27, 2016)

I once read a devotion on the Proverbs 31 Ministries website that talked about worry and anxiety.[3] One thing it said was that we should turn our worries into worship. When you start to feel anxious and know that anxiety is creeping its way back into your mind, then you need to worship. Take that worry or anxious thought, give it over to God, and just start praising Him through song.

When I read that devotion I wondered why I had never thought of that before. I can remember the first time I implemented this new strategy. It was amazing to see the anxious thoughts leave my head as I sang my heart out to our wonderful Savior. I worshiped and the worry disappeared.

The next step I took with the Lord was to remember His presence. In the Philippians passage, Paul writes, "The Lord is near" (Philippians 4:5b). God revealed to me that He never left my side. During all my struggles with anxiety attacks, God was there. He didn't abandon me and leave me to fend for myself. He was there. I just had forgotten He was.

Today I practice remembering His presence by being still. A lot of times when I feel anxiety coming on, it's because I am going full speed ahead without applying the brakes at all. I must be willing to sit still and just be in His presence. I like to find a quiet place, one where I know I won't have any interruptions: my back porch, in the church

3   Karen Ehman, "Turning Worry into Worship", accessed April 16, 2014, http://proverbs31.org/devotions/devo/turning-worry-into-worship/

sanctuary, my sitting room, or even by one of my favorite waterfalls. I sit still, talk with God and listen and am just there. This helps me to feel His presence. And when I am able to feel His presence in the peaceful times, I am able to remember His presence in the anxious times. I've practiced being in His presence so I know He is there at all times.

The next step I took with God was prayer. During the course of that year of anxiety attacks, I never stopped calling out for God. I prayed…and I mean a lot! However, I realized I was praying for God to take it away, which is not a bad thing to pray for. But, what I wasn't doing during these prayer times was allowing God to take control. I was trying to fight my way through the anxiety by myself. I had my fists up ready to take out anxiety when an attack came on. When it did arrive, my fists didn't stay up long because anxiety kicked my butt. I allowed it to control me without ever allowing God to fight for me. Basically, I didn't give God a chance. I stopped trying to control my anxiety-ridding plans, and instead focused on letting go and giving it over to God.

Thanksgiving was a step I never thought I would take on this journey with God as far as anxiety goes. Why in the world would I ever give thanks to God in the scariest moment of my life? But, as this passage in Philippians 4 says, we must show God our thankfulness.

I read an article during my anxiety years that mentioned keeping a gratitude journal. So I began doing that and it totally changed me. Every morning when I woke up (or even during the middle of the night when I woke up because of anxiousness), I got out my notebook and wrote down all the things I was thankful for. I would add to that list at the end of each day as well. The list of thanksgivings was so long and I began to give thanks to God for each thing. It's amazing to see the difference in yourself when you begin to do something as simple as thanking God.

With each of these steps I took with God, the dark anxiety cloud began to lift. And that anxiety was replaced by the peace of God. By rejoicing in God, remembering His presence, praying, and giving thanks, I was able to see God instead of seeing the anxiety that surrounded me. God's peace became the guard of my heart and my mind. I can picture God's peace inside my heart and my mind, surrounding them both, and not allowing Satan back in with his attempts to scare me through the change I was experiencing. The peace of God has won the battle and I now know how to conquer the fear of anxiety and change.

### Change Will Come

Change is going to happen in your life. It's inevitable. But, you can stop the fear of it with God's help. I know what you are saying: "Easy for you to say, Vanessa." Yes, it is easy for me to say because I have been through this fear of change and I have come out on the other side knowing God brought me through it.

If change is occurring in your life right now, just breathe. If you feel like you can't breathe because all this change is overwhelming, then walk outside and take several deep breaths. Breathe in the Holy Spirit and breathe out your fear.

Then go get your Bible and memorize Philippians 4:4-7. When we can speak God's Word over the anxiety in our lives, we will see Satan slither away like a snake, unable to hurt us through his anxiety attacks. And most importantly, we become victors in this battle when we allow God to take control.

### Rise Up Prayer

*Prince of Peace, we come before You as people who desire to be free of anxiety; people who are afraid of change and who long to find the peace that You give. Rise up, O Lord, and free us from the chains of anxiety that keep us from experiencing Your peacefulness. Help us to rejoice in You, remember Your presence, be filled with thanksgiving, and seek You in prayer. May Your Word open up the flowing waters of peace that You long to provide for each one of us. In Jesus' name, Amen.*

# 5

# SURROUNDED BY FIRE
## *Fear of Criticism*

*I*t was super hot in there. That furnace was filled with blazing flames. How did they get into this hot mess, anyway?

Shadrach, Meshach, and Abednego were thrown into the fiery furnace because of one thing: they didn't please the king. All the king asked was for them to bow down to the golden statue when they heard the instruments played. But they had a problem with that. They worshiped only one God, the Holy One of Israel. There was no way they were going to please some earthly king by bowing down to this golden statue he had created. They didn't care what happened to them.

Their knees might have been shaking and their voices might have been quivering when they told the king they wouldn't bow down, but they were not going to give into fear just to please this man. What he was asking everyone to do was wrong. They knew it deep down in their hearts. They had faith in God and believed in His power.

They had the nerve to tell the king that even if God didn't deliver them they would never bow down and worship his golden statue. They were feeling pretty bold when they said that, and possibly wondering where that boldness came from, considering this king was about to throw them into a fiery furnace. But they knew beyond a shadow of a doubt that God was the only God they would serve and they had to remain faithful to God just as He had remained faithful to them. No matter what was about to happen to them.

### *Pressure to Please Others*

Any time you start a new job there is pressure: to do well, to make an impression on your boss, for people to like you, to live up to what is required of you, to please everyone. When you work in the church there's not just one person you want to please, but many people. You want everyone in the church to like you and think that you do an awesome job.

Let's face reality here. You can't please everybody and not everyone is going to like you. It's just not going to happen. There will always be that one person or a group of people who don't like anything you do. It will happen.

I was eighteen months into a job when criticisms began to fly. When the pastor asks you to come to his office, it's not always a good thing. I don't remember all of the criticisms he shared with me. What I do remember is the hurt I felt. So much hurt and devastation. Here I was trying my best (or what I thought was my best) only to hear that people were not happy with the job I was doing. You called me here, Lord, so why isn't everything going perfectly?

The criticisms didn't stop at that meeting. Year after year, when I had my staff evaluations, something seemed to come up that I was doing wrong.

Even though I was a year into the job, I still had so many new things going on in my life. I had gotten married and within fifteen months had given birth to my first child. I struggled with working full-time, being a mom to a newborn, and being a good wife. There were some people in the church who saw I struggled and began to complain.

I didn't want to be a stay-at-home mom. That just wasn't me. I have a lot of respect for all the moms who do that. It's a very important job. But I wanted to continue what I felt the Lord wanted me to do. I wanted to be a Youth Director and share and teach about the Lord to all those wonderful teenagers at church. They were an awesome group of kids. I wanted to continue to love on them and nurture them in their faith journey.

So, how was I going to continue doing all that I do and please my family as well as the youth, parents, and congregation at my church? It seemed no matter what I tried, I couldn't win. I tried hard to do better and to be better, but somehow I wasn't pleasing people. What was I doing to make some people not like me?

When you are being attacked in your job, it is hard. What's worse is when you are serving God on staff at a church and you are being criticized by other Christians. These are people who love the Lord just as much as you do. People who worship with you every Sunday. I couldn't seem to grasp why I was receiving so much criticism. Why? What did these people have against me?

I felt like David when he wrote in Psalm 3:1:

"O Lord, how many are my foes! Many are rising up against me."

However, not everyone was against me. I learned that, really, only a small group of people were the ones who did not like the job I was doing. There were many adults who supported, loved, and encouraged me. But, I was letting the few that were against me take over my life.

In the years I was in ministry at this job, fear of criticism crept its way into my heart and set up base camp. This fear consumed me. I felt like I could not do anything right. I felt like my every move was being watched. If I messed up, then I would hear about it. I would get that phone call from the pastor to come down to his office.

Fear began to surround me like a fire. I was trapped in the middle of this burning blaze with no way out. The walls of flames were high and with every critical thing said about me it became harder and harder to see over that wall. I let this fear control me. I let it consume me. It became very hard to focus on the work God had given me to do.

All my mind could do was think about why there were people who didn't like the job I was doing.

My focus was not where it should have been. And that was exactly what Satan wanted. Nothing pleases Satan more than to take you off the task of what God has called you to do. Satan wants your focus off of God. He wants you to keep your mind preoccupied with other things. He enjoys watching you suffer through things because he believes you won't make it through. He likes making you feel like you are surrounded by fire with no way out.

### *The Fiery Furnace*

Life for me at that time felt much like what I believe Shadrach, Meshach, and Abednego went through when they were thrown into the fiery furnace. In Daniel 3, Nebuchadnezzar was angry. He didn't like these three men who were disobeying him by not falling down and worshiping him when the instruments sounded. He ordered them to be thrown into the furnace of fire. He actually was so enraged that he ordered the furnace to be heated seven times more than what was normal. Seven times! Talk about feeling the devil on your back.

They were bound together and thrown into the red hot fiery furnace. It was so hot that it killed the men who lifted Shadrach, Meshach, and Abednego into the furnace. I can't even begin to imagine the hotness of the fire. The only time I have been close to a blazing fire is around the campfire ring, and it's only blazing hot if you get really close to it. That doesn't compare to the hotness of that furnace.

Shadrach, Meshach, and Abednego were protected in the furnace. As soon as they were thrown in, King Nebuchadnezzar could not believe his eyes. Was he really seeing a fourth person in the fire with them?

These three men were bound, too. They were tied up so none of them could try to escape. The king did not want anyone to get out of there. How in the world could another person have gotten in that furnace? The king even said one of these men had the "appearance of a god" (Daniel 3:25).

Then Nebuchadnezzar throws open the furnace and yells for the men to come out. As they walk out of the furnace, everyone notices there is no sign of fire damage on them. There is no singed hair, no burnt clothes, and they didn't even smell like fire (Daniel 3:27).

No fire smell on them? How is that possible? Anyone who sits around a campfire will walk away with the scent of fire on their clothes, in their hair, everywhere. I can even go down the street to buy some boiled peanuts from the man on the side of the road, stand next to his big pot of boiling peanuts sitting on a fire for just a few minutes and get back into my car and smell like fire. So, how can three men who were thrown into a big fire, first of all, not smell like fire, and most importantly, not be burned at all?

There's only one way. They had the protection of God. And that is the same protection I found at last when I was in the "furnace of criticism". Inside the hot fire which seemed to consume my life, I found God's love and protection. I felt God's arms surround me with His love. I felt His presence very strongly. I found peace through His Word.

And just when I thought I was going to go down in this burning blaze, God whispers the words I need to hear:

"When you pass through the waters, I will be with you; and through the rivers, they shall not overwhelm you; when you walk through fire you shall not be burned, and the flame shall not consume you" (Isaiah 43:2).

Those words were the water that killed the fire for me. Those words brought down the burning flames that surrounded me. They cooled me off and reminded me of where my focus should be: on serving God. Those words were the protection I needed in that furnace.

There were two things I wanted to do when I felt like I was in the fiery furnace. The first was to cry anytime someone said something to hurt me. And, well, I did cry. Just ask my husband. He can tell you the many times I came home in tears. I became very sensitive and so tears just seem to easily flow.

But the tears were helpful. They helped me to release the anger I felt against others. They also helped me to feel God's presence. Psalm 56:8 (NLT) says:

"You keep track of all my sorrows. You have collected all my tears in your bottle."

Those wet tears, flowing down my face, extinguished the hot burning flames that surrounded me. They calmed me and reminded me that, no matter what anyone said, God loved me. They were a prayer to God when I could not speak. I know that God hears me. It was so comforting to know He collects my tears and knows all my sorrows, too.

The second thing I wanted to do was defend myself. I wanted people to know I was actually doing the best I could. I wanted to be perfect and I don't like not doing my best or having others think I am not good at something. So, anytime criticisms came against me, I felt like I had to defend myself.

I think defending yourself is a natural reaction. If you are being physically attacked, then you just aren't going to sit there and let them beat you up. You are going to fight back. I was being attacked by others through their words. My natural reaction was to defend myself by showing everyone I was not a bad Youth Director.

However, that did not seem to bring me comfort. It seemed like the more I spoke up for myself, the higher the flames rose. What I thought was helping me, ended up hurting me.

### *Finding Freedom*

I was so ready to be out of that furnace. It seemed to take forever, but I finally was able to get through and see the Lord and His amazing love for me.

The first step into walking through that fire was to forgive. I needed to forgive every single person who said something to hurt me. I had no clue who many of those people were, either. Usually when people complain about you in the church they don't go to you directly. They go to your pastor or a committee. But in order to move past this, I needed to forgive as Jesus did. And believe me, it was hard. I didn't want to forgive these people. I wanted to stay angry and bitter. I realized that in order to come out of that fiery furnace, I needed to forgive and love those who had hurt me.

I had forgiven and now I had to let it go. I couldn't focus on the pain I felt when I remembered the hurtful words spoken to me. I wanted to be free and I knew that letting it go was how I would find freedom from the pain.

The next step I took was to allow God to be my shield. This meant giving up control of my life. God's presence was there. God's love was there. God's protection was there. I could feel all of those things. But, I wasn't allowing God to fully do all of them. I thought I could solve my own problems. I could still love God and feel His presence, but I thought I could handle all the details of my life, including the fear I was feeling of being criticized.

What I received from the Lord was Psalms 3:3-4 (NIV). David writes:

"But you, O Lord, are a shield around me, my glory, the One who lifts my head high. I call out to the Lord, and he answers me from his holy mountain."

Isn't that a wonderful verse? God is our shield. He protects us from the fiery furnaces we are in. He protects us from the flaming arrows the devil likes to shoot at us. He is the one who lifts up our head and helps us see our way out.

I had to let go of control and allow God to do His job; I needed to let Him be my shield. God is there to protect me, to guide me, and to love me, but I had to let Him do those things without getting in the way. Do you know how hard that is, too?

When I learned how to forgive, to let go, and allow God to be my shield, I could feel the flames going out. I could see now. There was God. Plain as day. I had missed God because I was too focused on my fear of criticism.

God can take away your fear of criticism by just believing in Him, loving Him, and putting your total trust in Him. Don't let the fear you feel of criticism keep you from serving God. Don't let it keep you from doing that which He has called you to do.

God is there. He is your shield. He fights off the enemy for you. Let him take control of your life. Don't worry about what others think. Don't let your primary focus be pleasing people. Focus on God and what is pleasing to Him. When you allow God to control your life, He will simply amaze you.

### Rise Up Prayer
*Heavenly Father, we come before You with hurts that run deep. Criticism from others has thrown us into a*

*furnace that is blazing hot and our focus is off of You. Rise up, O Lord. Pull us from this furnace of fire and put out the fiery flames from the enemy. Be our shield. Help us give control over to You so we can fully serve You. In Jesus' name, Amen.*

# WHO'S IN CHARGE?
## *Fear of Authority*

*W*here was this guy anyway?

Moses had been gone for a very long time and we were getting tired of waiting around on him. We are the Israelites, God's people, the ones He delivered from slavery in Egypt. Why are we having to wait so long? He said he had to go talk to God up on the mountain, but he has been gone a long time. What is he actually doing up there?

We aren't so sure of his authority anymore. I mean, first of all, do we really have to listen to what he says? He takes us out of Egypt, out of a place where we were being fed nicely. Granted, we were slaves, but at least the meals were good! Here in the wilderness all we have to eat is manna and quail. Every. Day. It's getting a little old.

Then, we really aren't sure he knows where he is going. We feel like we have been walking in circles for a very long time. We know it's not that far to get to the land of Canaan from Egypt, but for some reason it's taking forever to get there. Are we lost? Maybe we need a better guide.

And now we feel abandoned. Someone who claims to be our leader has left us. Is he ever coming back? Did he get tired of our complaining and ditch us? Are we to fend for ourselves now out in this wilderness?

Moses says that he talks to God and that God is the true leader of us, but we have yet to see God. We wish that we had something to look at, like a statue, that represents God. We just want to be able to see God and be able to worship Him. It's hard to listen or worship what you cannot see.

I think we have come up with a plan, though. Since Moses is gone, and who knows when or if he will come back, then we will approach Aaron and coerce him into building a statue for us. Something that we can see and worship. Something that will be beautiful and will be our god. And then that statue will be our leader and we can follow it. We don't want to listen to Moses anymore.

### Rule Follower

All my life I have been a rule follower. If there was a rule, then I made sure not to go against it. When my mother told me not to see rated R movies, I didn't watch them (even when my friends went to see Roadhouse with Patrick Swayze and I had to go to a PG movie all by myself).

When my teacher told the class to be quiet, then I made sure not to talk to my friends. When my orthodontist told me to wear my headgear and retainer, then I wore it (even if I hated them both). When my basketball coach told us not to throw across the court passes, then I didn't (if we did then we would have to run guts, which I really despised). If my Sunday school teacher told me to memorize a Bible verse, then I did it (especially after she told us we would win a prize the next week if we could say it). If the speed limit is 45 mph, I make sure not to go more than five miles over that.

I followed these rules because I was told to by someone who had authority over me: parents, teachers, doctors, coaches, pastors, policemen, bosses. If anyone with authority over me tells me what to do, then I make sure I listen to them and follow exactly what they say.

Why do I do everything I am told? I guess you could call me a G-G (goodie-goodie). I do not want to disappoint anyone. I do not want anyone mad at me. I especially don't want the punishment that would incur if I didn't do what they said. It's like I have this fear of anyone who has authority over me. It was more a fear of what would happen if I didn't do what they said. If I disobey then I would get punished and I really don't want that.

### Authority in the Church

In the Methodist Church, pastors move around. When one pastor leaves, you get another one. However, your church doesn't decide who you will hire to be the new pastor. The Bishop and Cabinet of your conference appoint your church a pastor. You may think that's crazy, but a lot of prayer goes into these appointments and I can't even imagine all the work and stress the Cabinet feels when it's time for this every year. It's a hard job taking into consideration every pastor in the conference, their leadership style, their strengths and weaknesses, and their family situations. There is a lot of work that goes into consideration of new appointments and I am thankful to those who do this for our conference.

Having this type of system in the Methodist Church, you pretty much have to prepare yourself for any type of leadership. You don't know how a pastor will lead, but you have to trust and believe that God will be with your church and will give wisdom to the pastor as the authority of this particular congregation.

I have worked for many pastors and they all have different leadership styles: laid back, in charge, trusting, micromanagers, caring, and compassionate. None of them are the same and all lead the best way they know how.

With every pastor having their own leadership style, it is hard to know what to expect since they lead differently. Because of this, I developed a fear of authority. With the change of pastors every few years, I have had to adapt to a new leadership style quickly. Just when you get used to one leader, they leave and a new one comes in. It is hard, especially when you really like working with a pastor. I even went home and cried when one of the pastors I worked with told us he was leaving. He was a strong leader for our church, an excellent pastor, and one I enjoyed working with. He was the one who hired me for the job and when he told us he was leaving, fear immediately began to set in of the next person in authority at our church.

Fear often makes its initial debut into my thoughts as this: *Who will it be? Will they be a good leader? Will they like me? Will they think I do a good job? Will they be encouraging?* Then these anxious thoughts turn into worry. I sit and think about who will be our new pastor and then my mind starts worrying about situations and details that will more than likely never happen. That worry turns into stress and I am sweating it out every day leading up to the arrival of the new pastor. Then that stress likes to create health problems for me in the form of stomach issues, breathing problems, headaches, neck problems, and other things. All those anxiety issues like to creep their way back into my body any time fear arises.

Maybe this was how the Israelites felt too. They had to be going through some anxious times. They had a leader who pulled them out of slavery and was delivering them to the Promised Land. Yet there were times when they were unsure of his authority and leadership. They didn't like traveling in the wilderness nor did they like eating the same thing every day. All Moses seemed to be doing was walking them around in circles and sometimes he just up and disappeared on them. They did not like the authority Moses had and decided to create their own leadership... in the form of a golden calf. And we all know how that turned out for them. Not so good (see Exodus 32).

Sometimes anxiety, stress, and worry can cause us to do some crazy things. For the Israelites that was having Aaron form a golden calf for them out of their jewelry. For us, when it comes to being afraid of those in authority, that could mean saying something we shouldn't have said to our boss, complaining to others about our boss, or doing something we know we shouldn't do. And that could turn out for us much like it did for the Israelites...not good.

One day God led me to Romans 13. And that spoke directly to my heart. It was like this Bible passage was written just for me:

"Everyone must submit to governing authorities. For all authority comes from God, and those in positions of authority have been placed there by God. So anyone who rebels against authority is rebelling against what God has instituted, and they will be punished. For the authorities do not strike fear in people who are doing right, but in those who are doing wrong. Would you like to live without fear of the authorities? Do what is right, and they will honor you. The authorities are God's servants, sent for your good. But if you are doing wrong, of course you should be afraid, for they have the power to punish you. They are God's servants, sent for the very purpose of punishing those who do what is wrong. So you must submit to them, not only to avoid punishment, but also to keep a clear conscience" (Romans 13:1-5, NLT).

When I first read that verse I shouted out loud, *"Yes, Lord!"* I wanted to be free of my fear of authority. I did not want to be afraid of those who I work for. I wanted to enjoy the work I do and not be constantly worried about what my boss thinks of me or if I'm doing things right. I just wanted freedom from my fear of authority.

### Finding Freedom

I remember the time when I finally decided this fear was crazy and I needed to let it go. We had just gotten a new pastor. And of course I wanted to impress him and let him know that I was a hard worker and followed the rules (I know what you're thinking…she really is a goodie-goodie). As I was talking with him one day, he looked at me and told me he trusted me. I didn't have to get his approval for every little thing. I didn't have to tell him every little thing I was doing in my job. He said I was the director of my ministry and he trusted I would be a good leader. And he said he knew I was a good leader based on what the previous pastor had told him.

That moment was freeing. With those simple words he spoke, I could feel the ropes being cut off that weight a little. That moment was the start of my fear of authority burden being let go.

Letting go of a fear isn't always instantaneous. Just because I say in my mind that I want to let go of this fear doesn't mean it actually happens at that moment. My pastor's words were the beginning, but I learned a few important things through this passage in Romans 13 that helped me take the path that led to my freedom from this fear.

First of all, I was reminded that God is the ultimate authority and I must submit to Him. Am I afraid of God? Well, I don't want to be. But the reality of it is that I am at times afraid of God's authority. How scary is it to live a life totally trusting someone you cannot see? But that is where faith comes in. We need to realize that God is in control and His authority over heaven and earth is real. He is the author and perfecter of our lives. He writes only the best stories. We need to allow Him to write these stories for us, which involves submitting to His authority and trusting His best for us.

Second, I was reminded that I must submit to the governing authorities. Paul writes pretty clearly that we must do this (Romans 13:1). But, do we get a free pass from this if they aren't a good person? What if I think I'm right and they are wrong? What if they don't like me and I don't like them? Do I still have to submit to them?

That, of course, is a rhetorical question. Yes, you have to submit to them and listen to what they say. God knows best, even if we don't like what we are having to do.

Third, God showed me that my fear of authority comes from something I am not doing right. And for me, that something is a lack of trust in the authority He has given. Sometimes that is the hardest of these three reminders. When you have been hurt or criticized by authority, your ability to trust is affected. You don't want to trust someone who has hurt you. It's extremely difficult.

I always felt like I was tip-toeing around any boss I had. I was making sure to do everything right so I would please them. I wasn't one to rock the boat (or so I thought). I wanted to do everything they expected and more, so I would not upset them.

During all that time, though, I knew I was not trusting them. I wasn't trusting their judgment on things and I wasn't trusting anything they said. How could I, when I was afraid?

Most importantly, I knew I was not trusting God with this fear. I was not giving it over to Him. I was not allowing God to have access to this fear of authority. I thought I could handle it myself. I thought if I did everything right and followed all the rules then I could overcome it. If I could just show my boss I was perfect and did no wrong then all would be well, right?

God wanted me to first and foremost trust Him. Not myself and not someone else. But, just trust Him first. As Proverbs 3:5 (NIV) says:

"Trust in the Lord with all your heart and lean not on your own understanding."

I was using my own understanding and trying to control everything. I wasn't allowing God to be in control so He could show me how to let go and trust Him. When I realized this, I began to see how freeing it was to know God had this. If I would just trust Him first then I would be able to open up and trust the authority over me.

The fourth thing I needed to do was to forgive and let go of any past conflicts I had with any previous boss. And let me tell you, forgiveness is hard. Hurt is especially difficult to get over when it happens in the church. If you haven't ever experienced it, then I pray you never will.

Any time we are hurt by someone, we don't want to forgive. We want to stew over that situation for a very long time. We like to tell others how hard it was and how we couldn't believe what that person did to us. We like to play it over and over again in our heads and to others who will listen. And for what reason?

When we continue to think about and talk about the hurt someone else caused us, all we are doing is giving permission to the devil to keep hardening our hearts. We are saying forgiveness is not acceptable and so he takes that and turns it into bitterness. And when bitterness sets in it's even more difficult to forgive.

In Jeremiah 31, God plans to establish a new covenant with the people of Israel. The first one created under the leadership of Moses has been broken. This new covenant, though, will be stronger because it will help the people of Israel have a closer relationship with God; one in which they can know Him better. In this covenant God says:

> "For I will forgive their wickedness and will remember their sins no more" (Jeremiah 31:34, NIV).

I can only imagine the excitement of the Israelites. Hearing that God was no longer going to remember the bad things they do must be freeing for them. But, how was all this going to happen? Will God really forgive and not remember the things we have done?

The answer is a big yes. That yes comes in the form of Jesus. He was born here on earth for one purpose: to take on every sin, to bear the shame for each of us, and to die on the cross so that we could live forever with Him.

Jesus goes on to tell His disciples He is the new covenant. In Luke 22:20 Jesus says:

"This cup that is poured out for you is the new covenant in my blood."

The blood that Jesus shed on the cross for us is our sign of God's new covenant. Jesus is the new covenant. God never breaks His promises. He gave us Jesus to take away our sins.

And that is why, my friends, we should let go and forgive. Jesus died for us. Not just for one or two people, but He died for all of us. He forgives us of our sins and He does not remember them. Not at all. Our slate is wiped clean.

We need to follow Jesus' example and forgive those that hurt us and then forget about it. I know it will not be instantaneous. We're only human and it's hard to forgive and forget. But, I urge you to work on it every day. Work on erasing the bitterness or resentment that you so desperately want to hold on to. Let. It. Go.

I have held on to un-forgiveness in my heart and it has only caused me more pain. For a long time I carried around with me resentment for a person in authority. It was not good. It just made my life harder and darker.

One day God spoke to me. He showed me the un-forgiveness I was still carrying around with me about the person in authority. He reminded me that in order to move on and accomplish all He has for me then I needed to let go. I truly needed to forgive and forget.

### It's a Real Thing

Fear of authority is real for many people. We all have jobs and sometimes those in authority over us make it hard to do our jobs. Perhaps we don't like something they said or we don't like the way they handled a situation. Or maybe we don't care for the way they lead. But, that doesn't give us a valid reason to go and do the opposite of what they want us to do. It doesn't mean we can do what we want. And it especially does not mean we should be afraid of them.

Paul clearly states in Romans 13 that we are to have no fear of authority. These people in authority are God-appointed. If we do good, then we will receive their approval. If we allow the anger, resentment, and bitterness we feel toward them because of something they did, we are only causing more harm for ourselves. If you find it hard to submit to authority, then I urge you to seek freedom from it by remembering Romans 13. When you do, I believe you will find that your fear of authority will begin to fade.

Your burden will be lifted and you can continue to walk in the way of the Lord.

### *Rise Up Prayer*

*Father God, You are the ultimate authority in our lives. You love us unconditionally and You know what is best for us. But, Lord, You know there are times when we question You and are frightened of the way You are calling us. And we are the same way with people You have put in authority over us. We know, Lord, that is not right and we repent for that. So now we ask You to rise up, O Lord. Free us from this fear we have of those in authority over us. Break through the bitterness that holds tightly inside our hearts and keeps us from forgiving those who have hurt us. And most importantly, may we also trust You as the one who reigns as the authority over heaven and earth. In Jesus' name, Amen.*

---— 7 —---

# WHO ARE YOU?
## *Fear of Not Being Good Enough*

D avid wasn't afraid of anything. He was a shepherd. And shepherds had to do some courageous things when it came to protecting their sheep. He had killed lions with his bare hands. He would do anything for his sheep. He was fearless.

So when he came to visit his brothers on the battlefield, he couldn't believe that not one single person was out there fighting the giant, Goliath. Inside he was laughing because he thought all of these men were chicken. Scaredy cats. What was wrong with them? They were soldiers for crying out loud. Soldiers were expected to be brave and fight anything or anyone. But for some reason, all of the Israelite soldiers were hiding out in their tents!

David decided it was time for him to step up and show these soldiers how it's done. He didn't care that Goliath was a massive giant. He didn't care that he was just a boy and Goliath was much older than him. He didn't care that he didn't have any soldier armor or even a weapon. He had something much better. He had God. And David knew that God would be with him.

But why is everyone laughing at him? Why are his brothers embarrassed by him? Why does Saul think he is too young? Forget all they are saying and doing. He was going to kill that giant and he would do it with the weapons he could use best.

David knew he was good enough, despite what others were saying. He knew he could do it. Finally he was given the chance to show how good he was. And you know what happened…he killed that giant.

### *Where It All Started*

I love basketball. It has always been my favorite sport. I love the fast pace of the game: running down the court, dribbling the ball, looking up to make the perfect pass, squaring up and following through, stealing the ball away from another player. It's an exciting and thrilling sport.

I began playing basketball when I was around eight years old. My mom decided to put me in a basketball clinic at a local elementary school so I could learn the basic fundamentals of the game. I fell in love with basketball there.

I played basketball for a team from then on. Elementary years were spent playing on a team for our local Park & Rec. When I hit middle school I tried out for the school team and made it both years. We had a good team. Many of my friends also played on the team and that made it more fun. We laughed a lot those years and had fun together.

When I began high school I tried out for the JV team and made it. I was thrilled! This would be a great start to my high school career. I loved basketball and just knew I would be playing a lot and would do well.

In the beginning of the season, we conditioned with the Varsity team. Talk about being intimidated. I was nervous, shy, and sometimes afraid to be around those juniors and seniors. We were running on the football field one day, pushing it hard in the hot sun. Suddenly a sharp, burning pain shot through my upper thigh. The pain brought me to a screeching halt. I screamed out and immediately fell to the ground. Everyone seemed to stop running, too. All eyes were on me and I did not like it.

As everyone watched and stared at me, my coach and the Varsity coach came over to check on me. They took one look and knew what I had done. Pulled muscle. The pain was bad. I couldn't run, much less walk. How was I going to play basketball now?

My coach got ice and wrapped it around my upper thigh. He showed compassion when I was in pain. He told me what I needed to do to help heal my muscle. I hoped this injury would heal quickly and I could get back to playing my favorite sport soon.

As I lay there on the ground, the Varsity coach decided to make an example out of me. She told the rest of the players that this is what happens when you don't condition well. If you don't exercise and get in shape then you're going to end up like this: pulled muscles and not able to play.

Her words stung. For someone who doesn't like to be the center of attention, I was all of a sudden in the spotlight. But, for the wrong reasons. I didn't want to be an example to others, especially when I was hurting or in pain. I felt ashamed and bad for not conditioning myself better. I felt like I was not good enough to play on this team.

As the season began, I noticed I was being more of a benchwarmer than a player. My friends were getting playing time, but I seemed to sit on the sidelines cheering on my team more than I would like to have done. I was getting frustrated because I wasn't getting enough playing time. My mother told me I should go talk to the coach and ask why I wasn't playing more. I remember being so scared to ask him why I wasn't playing much and how I could change that. No one likes to have to ask a coach why he doesn't play you. It could only mean one thing...you aren't that good.

I knew I wasn't as great a player as some of my friends on the team, but I really loved basketball and wanted to play. I don't remember the actual conversation I had with him, but what I remember from that conversation was that he cared. He wasn't a coach that dismissed the weaker players because they weren't as good. He cared about each of his players and wanted them to get better.

That season I spent extra time in practice. I practiced with the team first, and then I stayed afterwards and my coach worked with me on shooting and I also did extra drills. I worked hard. I wanted to improve and do better. It paid off. I got more playing time.

I don't even remember what our team record was. Did we win more than we lost? Who knows. What I do remember from that season, though, is a coach that believed in me. He cared enough about his players to work with them to help them improve and be a better player. He taught me to believe in myself and be confident, which is something I was lacking as a 14-year old. He taught me, most importantly, that I am good enough.

### Who Says

I remember a song by Selena Gomez called "Who Says". (Don't judge me. I have kids and we listened to that song when it was out). In this song she talks about beauty and others making you feel like you aren't beautiful or good enough. She keeps asking, "Who says?" One lyric says:

*"You made me insecure, told me I wasn't good enough."*

I believe that our fear of being good enough comes from two places: from others or from ourselves.

People can be mean. And I'm not really sure why. Why do people desire to strike you down so hard with just the use of the words that roll off their tongue? It's amazing how those few words can cut you in half. You might be on cloud nine and feeling so confident about yourself and what you are able to do, then along comes a person to slash through that cloud and drop you all the way to the ground. Words from others can damage your self-esteem. They can make you afraid of doing what you want to do, what you love to do, and what you are really good at doing.

### David is Good Enough

The story of David defeating Goliath is a good example of someone who rises above the words of others (1 Samuel 17). David is the youngest of eight sons of Jesse from Bethlehem. His three oldest brothers have joined the army of King Saul and have gone off to battle with the Philistines. Their battle was taking place in a small town called Socoh, which was about fourteen miles west of Bethlehem.

During this time of battle, David's father asked him to deliver food to his brothers (1 Samuel 17:17-18). I can only imagine that David really enjoyed getting to do this errand for his father. First of all, he wasn't old enough to be in the army. According to Numbers 1:20, every male had to be at least 20 years old to go to war. Even though the Bible does not say, we can assume that David was younger than 20 since he was not in Saul's army. This errand is David's chance to see his older brothers and possibly even watch some of the battle take place. What young boy wouldn't want to see some fighting?

Remember that Socoh is about fourteen miles from Bethlehem. So, how long would it take for David to walk to Socoh? The average person walks about three miles per hour, so it would have probably taken around five hours for him to walk this distance, unless he decided to run, of course. Fourteen miles is a long way, especially just to deliver some food and pop in for a visit with his brothers to see how the battle is going.

David happens to arrive at the Israelites camp just when they are getting ready to go to the battle line, shouting the war cry (1 Samuel 17:20). David finds his brothers and begins talking with them. About that time, Goliath comes out and starts shouting the same words he has spoken for the past forty days, which is basically challenging the Israelites to send someone to fight him. But, no one in Saul's army is willing and ready to go fight that massive, mean giant.

David hears Goliath talking and then turns to some of the men and says in 1 Samuel 17:26b:

"For who is this uncircumcised Philistine that he should defy the armies of the living God?"

His oldest brother, Eliab, overhears him and gets angry. He scolds him for even coming to the battlefield and for leaving the sheep that he is supposed to be attending, asking him who is keeping watch over them. I can just hear this brother's tone: frustrated and annoyed. Eliab has been embarrassed by the words of his youngest brother. He probably wants to crawl under a rock and hide because his brother has shown up, out of the blue, and said the dumbest thing ever. Eliab is frustrated with David because he thinks he knows everything and is good enough to be a soldier. Who is he to even think he knows such things? He is just a young boy.

David's response to Eliab is the classic little brother response because he doesn't understand:

"What have I done now? It was only a question?"
(1 Samuel 17:29).

I know what it's like to have an older sibling frustrated with you and to be embarrassed to be seen with you. It just comes with being a teenager. It's like you are supposed to feel this way toward your sibling. You are the older sibling and you know everything and the one thing you are sure of is that your younger sibling is not good enough to do those things that you are able to do (by the way, I love my older sister very much!).

David didn't have the support of his siblings because he wasn't old enough and wasn't wise enough to know the ins and outs of being a soldier and fighting in a battle, especially against someone as huge as Goliath. David's brothers already had their minds made up. He wasn't good enough because of his age.

However, David did not let that stop him.

Some of the other soldiers took what David said and repeated them to Saul. Saul was intrigued enough because he invited David to come see him. After having no one step up to the plate for the past forty days, Saul wanted to hear what David had to say.

David told Saul he was ready. He would go and fight this Philistine (1 Samuel 17:32). Now, can you imagine what Saul might have done when David said this to him? He probably smiled and then busted out laughing. Everyone was probably thinking the same thing that Saul said to David:

"You are not able to go against this Philistine to fight with him; for you are just a boy and he has been a warrior from his youth" (1 Samuel 17:33).

Saul doesn't think David is good enough because he is just a boy.

Those words probably angered David. *Who are these people to think that I can't fight this Philistine?* No one else was stepping up to the plate to fight him so why not let him? So, he fires back with his resume. He is a shepherd, but not just any shepherd. He doesn't just tend to the sheep, feed them, and make sure they are kept safe. He has killed for these sheep. He has fought off lions and bears and saved his sheep. Goliath is going to be like one of these lions and bears because he has defied the armies of the living God (1 Samuel 17:36).

Saul didn't think David was good enough because of his age. What boy could fight a giant like Goliath? This boy was crazy. Didn't he know he would be killed? Maybe Saul was tired of fighting against David and telling him he was too young. Or maybe Saul was convinced by David's amazing display of his skills. Finally Saul said yes and offered this piece of advice: "Go, and may the Lord be with you!" (1 Samuel 17:37). Saul was probably really saying good luck…you're going to need it.

David walks out to face Goliath with just a sling and a few stones he picked up from the wadi (the valley). He tried wearing the fancy, heavy gear that all soldiers wear but couldn't even walk in it. He wasn't comfortable. He wanted to use the weapons he was familiar with; the ones he knew he could use well. And for him, that was a sling and some stones.

Goliath took one look at David and was angry. The Bible says: "When the Philistine looked and saw David, he disdained him, for he was only a youth, ruddy and handsome in appearance" (1 Samuel 17:42). He was upset because the Israelites sent this little scrawny, handsome boy to come and fight him. It probably was seen as an insult to him. Goliath even asks, "Am I a dog, that you come to me with sticks?" (1 Samuel 17:43).

I mean, think about it, how would you feel if the enemy you were fighting sent someone that was way smaller than you; someone that didn't even compare to your fighting ability. You would probably be insulted, too. You would want at least a little bit of competition as you fought. And I'm sure that's what Goliath wanted, too. He had been waiting forty days for a good fight. He was ready to win. He wanted to show the Israelites how powerful and strong he truly was. But instead, they sent out this little boy whom he knew he could squash with one step of his foot.

Goliath didn't think David was good enough to fight him. He was just a boy for crying out loud. Goliath had been training as a soldier since he was a boy. He learned how to be a great warrior from having years of training. David had no training at all. He wasn't even wearing the normal attire of a soldier. How could this little boy be good enough to fight him?

David is not afraid. He talks some good smack to Goliath (I can only imagine the smirk on Goliath's face as he does). Then he ran quickly toward the giant, took a stone out of his bag, put it into the sling and slung it. That small stone struck the giant so hard on his forehead that it killed him. And just like that, this little boy had defeated the giant that had everyone running for the hills.

David was told he was not good enough by three different people: his brother, King Saul, and Goliath. All of these people told him he was just a boy. He was not able to be a good soldier because of his age. He was just a young shepherd boy, with no training at all. There was no chance of him even being a soldier now because he was too young.

What if David had actually listened to all of these people and didn't stand up to fight Goliath? I wonder how long the Israelites and Philistines would have stayed there waiting on someone to be brave enough to fight Goliath? Would the Israelites have even won or would they have become slaves of the Philistines?

I am glad that David didn't let the words of these people stop him. He was determined to show them he was good enough. David knew in his heart that he had the wisdom and skills to fight this giant. He knew he could do it. He wasn't going to let the mocking and degrading keep him from conquering that crazy, mean old giant. Thank you, God, for David's courage, bravery, and confidence.

### Confidence in Ministry Shattered

In the ministry, my confidence has been shaken too. When people criticize you for the work you do in the church, you question yourself. You say things like: *Maybe I'm not good enough. Am I even doing the right thing?*

And then you question God's calling. You wonder if you heard God right. Maybe you thought God was saying one thing, but really He meant something else. Your mind begins spitting out excuse after excuse about why you shouldn't do the thing God wants you to do. If other people criticize the job you are doing, then God is probably doing the same thing, right?

Get out of this mindset, friends! It's not good. Satan is attacking you right where he knows it will get you. He throws lies into your thoughts to make you feel like you aren't good enough. He hurls evil and hurtful words into the hearts of others to speak to you. He will do any and everything to make you believe you aren't any good. Don't believe the lies. Fight back.

### Fighting Back

In one corner is Satan. In the other corner it's you. As you look around, the crowd is cheering. They are shouting your name. They are clapping and going crazy. They want you to win.

But then you look over at the other corner to see Satan laughing at you, mocking you, and telling you that you aren't good enough. You won't win. He will defeat you.

You start to feel overwhelmed and are ready to throw in the towel before you even fight. It's too much. Satan is right. You just aren't good enough.

And then you hear that still small voice. It seems to be louder than the crowd in the room. It's like that voice is on speaker inside your heart and you can hear it perfectly.

*You are good enough. I love you. Don't listen to Satan. Listen to me.*

And then God speaks something you just can't ignore:

"My grace is sufficient for you, for power is made perfect in weakness" (2 Corinthians 12:9).

That's all you need to get up, turn around, and knock the living day lights out of Satan. With every punch you throw, you are shouting praises to God, telling Satan you are good enough, screaming at the top of your lungs the name of Jesus (because, as my grandmother always said, Satan runs at the sound of His name.) And with that, Satan is knocked out and he disappears. Gone for now. He'll be back, I'm sure, but you know how to knock him out again so you are armed and ready to fight.

### *Finding Freedom*

Freedom from this fear is hard work. Satan's lies in your head speak loud inside your heart and your head. I believed them for a long time. I didn't think I was good enough, especially when it came to serving the Lord. Why would God choose me to do His work? Didn't He know I wasn't good enough?

But I finally got tired of hearing those lies from Satan and found freedom from this fear of not being good enough. God showed me three ways I can overcome this fear with His help.

The first step is to know God's Word. Nothing scares Satan like the Word of the Lord. When you study and memorize Scripture then you are armed and ready for those attacks. Find Scripture that speaks to you for those lies of not being good enough. Then when Satan comes back with his fiery arrows of lies, you can speak God's Word and allow it to deflect the arrows that Satan continuously throws at you.

The second step is one I have found helpful my whole life: post Scripture around your house. Why not see God's Word alive in your house? Find your favorite Scriptures and post them all around your home. In every room, hang His Word where you will see it and be reminded of it and speak it if necessary to ward off the enemy.

When I was in college, I wrote down my favorite Bible verses on construction paper and hung them up all over my dorm room. Seeing God's Word every day in that room helped me so much in those fun, but difficult years of college life. And I still hang Scripture around my house today: in my bedroom, living room, kitchen, and even next to my desk. I want to be able to see the Word of God and know that I have the tools for fighting off the enemy posted around my house.

The third step is to believe. Satan's lies like to break the faith we have in Jesus. They make us doubt God and our ability to do the work He has called us to do. But, we must continue to believe. Believe you are God's child. Believe that "I can do everything through Christ who gives me strength" (Philippians 4:13, NLT). Believe in the unending love of our Savior.

One of the ways I continue to remember to believe is by seeing that word every day. A friend at church gave me a yellow card with the word "believe" on it. I chose to put that card on the dashboard in my car. I'm in my car multiple times a day and whenever I sit in the driver's seat, I look over at that bright yellow card and am reminded of my belief in God the Father, Son, and Holy Spirit. I'm reminded to always believe in myself and the gifts God has given me.

I listened to the lies that I'm not good enough for too long. I was finally tired of hearing it and decided to break free of that fear. I did not want to be burdened by fear and let it keep me in hiding.

Are you ready to fight back? Are you ready to slap Satan in the face with the Word of the Lord? Are you ready to stand up and say "I am good enough!" I know you are. So let's break this chain that keeps us from standing. Let's get rid of this fear. Cut loose the fear of not being good enough. Tell Satan you are good enough because you believe in Jesus Christ! Rise up and let it go so you can be the person God created you to be.

### *Rise Up Prayer*

*Precious Lord, we know You created us and everything You created is good. For too long we have been misguided by Satan into thinking we are worthless and not any good; that we are especially not good enough to serve You. And we know that this thinking has to stop. Rise up, O Lord. Fight this battle for us. Take the lies Satan throws at us and knock them out of our hearts for good. May we study Your Word daily so we can stand up against the enemy when he returns. Keep us focused on Your promises. Help us to remember we are good enough because of Jesus Christ. We ask all these things in His holy name, Amen.*

# SEND ME...I THINK

## *Fear of Moving*

"By faith Abraham obeyed when he was called to set out for a place that he was to receive as an inheritance; and he set out, not knowing where he was going" (Hebrews 11:8).

Serving God has definitely been and will continue to be a journey of not really knowing where I am going. At times, that has been very scary. Am I strong enough, wise enough, and brave enough to have the faith of Abraham and leave my home, not knowing what way I am really going?

But isn't that what a life of serving God is like? Aren't we the crazy ones who pack up and move when God calls? I can plan all I want (and believe me, I try to do that because I am such a planner), but my direction is ultimately guided by the Lord. Now, don't get me wrong...I do my fair share of arguing with God and trying to squirm my way out of moving. Why? Because moving can be a frightening experience.

Since I graduated from high school I have moved six times: college, seminary, camp job, first youth ministry job, second youth ministry job, and children's ministry job. That's a lot of moving for a girl who spent the first eighteen years of her life in one city and in one home. All of these moves involved a lot of praying and a lot of faith. And I mean *a lot* of faith. But that doesn't mean I wasn't afraid of the process. I was anything but confident. I was a terrified girl who put on a front of excitement, happiness and readiness for the next adventure.

As much fun as each move would bring, I wondered if my faith and trust in God was strong enough to move in order to pursue this next step. Was there someone else I could learn from who also had a huge faith in God and they moved everything to start fresh somewhere new?

Why yes there is…none other than Abram, of course.

### Abram's Move

At the time of Abram's calling, he and his wife, Sarai, and his nephew, Lot, were living in the land of Haran. His father had just passed away. And then God spoke to Abram at the age of 75 and said:

> "Go from your country and your kindred and your father's house to the land that I will show you" (Genesis 12:1).

Abram was a man who had great faith in God, but do we think Abram had the boldness to listen?

Absolutely.

Abram's faith in God was pretty big. But, I wondered if he was scared? Surely he was. I mean, who doesn't get a little scared when it comes to moving? Was there a tiny ounce of fear in Abram? I would like to think there was because he was only human.

As I was reading the story of Abram's move, I began to see the different reasons why I am afraid to move. His story helped to shed some light on the different aspects of this fear of mine.

### The Call to Move

In Genesis 12:1, Abram is being called by God to move. God told him he would have to leave his country and all his people behind. Talk about a big move! Everything Abram has known for his entire life, he will have to leave. No friends and the only family coming were Lot and Sarai. The familiar things he had grown to love would no longer be in his sight or even within his reach. Everything would be new. And the craziest part of this call to move was that he had no clue where he was even going.

As I sit here and think about what God had asked Abram to do, all these questions pop up in my mind and I wonder if Abram was thinking the same thing: *Where will I get food? What about water to drink? Where will I live? How will I know where I should settle? Will the people in my new city be nice? Will they think I am crazy for listening to God and just going? What about my animals? Do I take them or leave them? I wonder how long it will take to get there? Can my wife make this journey? Does she think I am crazy? Does she trust me because I trust God? Does she trust God?*

The Bible does not seem to give us even the slightest detail about what Abram was thinking during all of this. I sure wish it did, though. Maybe then I would be able to see the fear that Abram had. I know it had to be there, even if it was just the tiniest bit of fear. He had to be afraid. I mean, he just had to be.

When God called Abram, it said He spoke to him and told him. God usually did the audible voice thing back in the Old Testament. Not so much these days, though. But, we do know when God speaks to us. How? Because everywhere we turn, we are hearing the same message over and over: from the Word, in a sermon, in a devotional, in a song, from another person. It's everywhere. God wants to make sure we get it. God wants us to do only one thing when He calls us to move, and that is to obey Him.

### Obedience Without Doubt

One thing I struggle with is determining whether or not I am hearing God correctly. Is that really God calling or is that my own desire? God desires obedience from each of His children. And that's the one thing I desire to do. I want to be obedient. I want to move where He calls. But I have a hard time with one thing…doubt.

Doubt is not something you seem to hear from Abram. I don't think there was once a time when he said, *"Oh man,*

*I don't know about this anymore, God. I think I might have misunderstood what you were saying to me. I think I'll turn around and go back to Ur. It's comfortable and it's safe and I know everybody there. That's what I think I should I do."* No, you don't hear any mention of that. He's all faith and no doubt. He's a man that didn't seem to question what God was wanting him to do. He just went. And he did it without any doubt.

Every time I moved, I know there was doubt and fear. I did not always have the faith of Abram. I worried about all the people I would meet and the city I was moving to. Will they like me? Will they think I am a good person and know what I am doing in my job? What about this new city? Where is the nearest grocery store? Is it a safe area? How will I know what area of the city is safe? Will I be able to find a house or apartment I can afford that's in a safe neighborhood? So many questions.

Did I have ultimate faith in God to go without doubting? You can answer that one for me. I wish I could say I did, but I cannot. I want so badly to tell you I had Abram's faith. Unfortunately, I fell short of it. But what I can tell you is that with each move, my faith got a little stronger and my doubt and fear got a little smaller. I came to realize God was with me in every move and He took care of every single detail.

### God Promises Blessings

God has called Abram and told him to leave everything behind and go to a new country, one God would show him. I love how in the next verses of Genesis 12, God takes away any doubt from Abram by promising several blessings. God says:

> "I will make of you a great nation, and I will bless you, and make your name great, so that you will be a blessing. I will bless those who bless you, and the one who curses you I will curse; and in you all the families of the earth shall be blessed" (Genesis 12:2-3).

What an amazing blessing. And that's not just one blessing. That's five blessings from God...five! God will bless Abram if he's obedient to leave everything behind and go to a place unknown. All he has to do is move.

What I find so cool is that God never asks anything of us without showing us He is faithful and will bless us. How many times have you been obedient to God and from your obedience blessings flow?

In every move I have made, I can see blessings from the Lord. At the time, those blessings may not have been very clear to me. God didn't tell me all the blessings I would receive. But now I can look back and see God's blessings in every single place He called me.

In the move to college, He blessed me with great friends, excellent professors, a place to work at the college and still be able to focus on my studies, some of the best ladies to work with at that college job, and a church camp where I could work during the summers, which happened to be the place that God used to call me into the ministry.

In the move to Durham to attend seminary at Duke, the blessings continued. On the second day of school I met the girl who would become my closest friend during my seminary years. She then introduced me to more people she had met and that group of friends became a close-knit group who did everything together and loved and supported one another, even to this day. God blessed me with wisdom so I could understand all I was learning (it was not always easy). God blessed me with an on-campus job so I could earn a little income while attending school. God also blessed me with a summer internship where I could experience first-hand the ins and outs of working in a church and on a church staff.

And I have to add that God gave me an extra special blessing during my time at Duke. He blessed me with tickets to the Duke Men's Basketball games. I won tickets both years I was there through the Graduate Student lottery system. What an incredible blessing to be able to experience the excitement of Duke basketball! The extra, extra special blessing came in my last semester in 2001 when the Duke Men's basketball team became National Champions! A very cool bonus blessing from God, as I like to call it.

In my move to my first real job to be the Faith Formation and Retreat Ministries Coordinator at a camp in North Carolina, I had to look hard for these blessings, as the loneliness clouded my vision. Those blessings definitely were not evident in my time there, but I can now see God and His work in that job.

God blessed me with a beautiful place to live for a year and in an awesome house. I lived right on the Pamlico Sound. The house was huge and had a boat dock, too. Peacefulness surrounded the quaint neighborhood and the water was a good place to spend afternoons alone, which I obviously got to do a lot of since I was so lonely. God blessed me with a friend I worked with who was so down-to-earth and made me laugh. She kept me smiling even when I didn't feel like being happy. God blessed me with my very first opportunity to write lessons for the campers. I worked with a friend to lead the Bible study activity the campers attended daily. Even though I never wrote any of those lessons down on paper, it gave me the experience I needed in planning fun activities for kids centered around a daily Bible story, which is what I do a lot of today in my job as a Children's Ministry Director. It took me a while to recognize those blessings, but God was more than gracious to supply me with them.

In my move to Charlotte as my first job as a Youth Director in a church, I was blessed with some of the best teenagers to work with. They were funny, eager to learn about God, and faithful in coming to activities. I was blessed with a pastor who guided me in my first church job and his wife, a co-worker as well, who helped me learn more about the day to day duties on a church staff. Even though I did not meet many friends my age while I was there, God did bless me with one couple my age who were so kind.

They took me in and let me hang with their family. It was also in Charlotte where God blessed me with Andrew, my husband. A man I have known since elementary school, but whom I never even thought of dating till I was living in Charlotte. God's timing is always perfect.

In my move to my second youth ministry job, God blessed me with another great group of teenagers, parents who were willing to help and be involved in the youth ministry, a Sunday school class filled with some of our dearest friends now, two daughters that were born during our time there, and a special couple who were our role models as parents; they have and continue to inspire us to be the best spiritual providers for our children.

In this last move to my first children's ministry job, God blessed me with a church that truly exhibits the body of Christ. He gave me two senior pastors who have encouraged and supported me in my ministry. He blessed me with the best staff I have ever worked with. He blessed me with a growing children's program that includes some pretty awesome kids and parents. He also blessed me with a new passion I have found in writing and encouraging others. Another blessing has been the three small groups that we have been a part of. Having a group of adults whom you can grow in your faith with is a gift. God has blessed us with some dear friends who are our spiritual guides and prayer warriors. And then there is the huge blessing of wonderful schools for my daughters and a house that is perfect for our family.

All these blessings (and many more that would take forever to write), have been provided by God because I was obedient to move where I felt He was leading. What if I had not listened? What if I had missed out on these blessings because of my fear to move? I am sure God would have blessed me in other ways had I stayed put, but I would have missed out on these particular blessings.

What if Abram hadn't listened to God? What would have become of him? We can be grateful for the example Abram gave us in his faithfulness and his obedience to go where God leads, even if it means packing up and leaving behind all you know.

### Giving Up Everything

I think probably the hardest part of moving, and what causes me the most fear is having to give up everything that has been my home and my comfort. That includes friends I have made, a house I have grown to love and called home, a place of work which I have enjoyed, and just the sense of peace and comfort you feel when you are at home.

I wouldn't call myself a homebody either. I'm not a person who longs to be at home all the time. I have always been kind of an adventurer and love going to new places and doing new things. I was the child who happily waved good-bye to her parents when they dropped her off at summer camp. No homesickness for me.

But there is a huge difference in missing home while away on vacation or summer camp and missing home because you have given up what was once your home to move to a new place God has called you to. And this fear of moving I had might even surprise some people, especially my mom and sisters who liked to joke that I am the black sheep of the family because I never got upset when I had to be away from them. That kind of homesickness was only temporary; I knew I was coming back soon. But the moving away from home was permanent.

I wonder if Abram had any problem with giving up his home and all the comfort it brought? Did he cry when he left? Was he sad? Did he have a huge attachment to his home or his land? What about his friends? Was he close to anyone he had to leave behind?

I can tell you that giving up all you have and know to follow God is extremely difficult; probably the most difficult thing about moving. But, in order to live a life sold out for God we must give up everything. We must be willing to leave behind what we call home and boldly move, even if it is sad and tears flow as we drive away. All the things we are going to miss will be replaced with new homes, new friends, and a new sense of comfort. Let God be enough. He is more than enough and He can and will provide all you need as you sacrifice and move for Him.

### Support of Family

I firmly believe when God calls you to move, He doesn't just call you, but He calls your family: your spouse and your children. When your family is willing to pack up and leave everything behind for you as you obey God, you know you are doing what the Lord is asking.

For four of my six moves, I didn't have a spouse or children to think about. It was just me, myself, and I. Moving wasn't too hard of a decision because all I had to think about was myself. I didn't worry about whether or not this move was going to affect anyone else. Those moves weren't as stressful as the last two moves I have made.

The last move we made was probably the first time I truly felt the Lord's calling on both me and my family. It was about eight years ago and I had wanted to find a job in Children's Ministry for a couple of years, but hadn't found anything. Then, out of the blue a friend tells me about a job at my current church. When I told my husband, he was pretty adamant that he was not moving. He liked where we lived and had no desire to move to a city an hour north of Atlanta. But then he went for a run (which is something he loves to do and it's also the time where he and God talk). And that's when God spoke to him. He came back from that run with a totally different perspective from when he left. He said he also felt God calling us to go to that city.

My kids were three and six at the time so moving at that point was pretty easy. They were not attached to anything and were actually excited about moving to a new place and getting a new house. It was an adventure for them and they were ready for it.

Having the support of my husband and children lifted the weight of fear off of my shoulders. Gone were the feelings of guilt because I was making our family move. Their support meant the world to me. Their support was yet another sign this move was ordained by the Lord.

When Abram got the call to move, the Bible says Lot and Sarai went with him (Genesis 12:5). Now, why would Lot, his nephew, be willing to support him in this move? Well, let's remember that Lot's father, Haran, died before they even moved from their original home in Ur. And when they settled in the land of Haran, Abram's father, Terah passed away. Gone were his father and grandfather. I am sure that Lot was like a son to Abram and Lot felt like Abram was a father to him. I can only assume they had grown close during their times together in Ur and Haran. Lot would naturally want to go where Abram, the only family living anywhere nearby, was being called. He supported Abram by moving with him.

Sarai was Abram's wife and she followed him no matter where he went. In 1 Peter 3:6, it says that Sarai called Abram "lord". Abram was her master and she served him with her whole heart. Wives were submissive to their husbands and saw their husbands as the head of the family. Wherever he went, she would follow. So, really, Sarai didn't have much choice in whether she was going to follow him or not. I guess she could have defied him and said she wasn't moving, but where else would she go? Abram was her family and she supported him and the decisions he made for them. And that meant supporting him when God called them to move.

Having the support of your family when God calls you to move helps alleviate the fear of moving. Gone are the feelings that you could be ruining your family's life and forcing them to go where you believe God is calling. I firmly believe, though, that when God calls you, He won't just call you. He'll call your family, too. He will take care of every single detail and the fear that has been gripping you when it comes to this aspect of the move, will be gone.

### The Welcome Team

Wherever God is calling you to move, one of the things you might fear, too, are the people you will meet: neighbors, work colleagues, church members. Will these people be nice? Will they like me? Will I like them? Will they be easy to work with or will I have a hard time getting along with them? Will my neighbors be good people or will I have to listen to loud music, yelling and fighting? What about the church members? Will they be accepting of me or will they criticize every single thing about me? These are all questions that may be running through your mind when you are preparing to move.

In my move to Charlotte, I experienced a welcome team that was amazing. I was still single so my moving team consisted of my mother, sisters, brother-in-law, and nephews. We had driven over four hours in a U-Haul and several cars. You know when you move yourself (without the assistance of a moving company), the last thing you want to do when you arrive is to unload everything from the U-Haul. You're just really tired from all that packing and driving. You need a good nap.

The church where I would be working wanted to help us unload. We gave them an estimated time of arrival and when we pulled into the apartment complex where I would be living there were so many teenagers and parents ready to help us that I could not believe my eyes. They waved and shouted and clapped like they were so happy to see me. I had never received a welcome like this before.

As I climbed out of the U-Haul and opened the door, I really did not have to do anything except point the direction of where to put the boxes. They were eager to help and unloaded every single box. They even brought food for us so we didn't have to try to find a place to eat. Our dinner and breakfast for the next morning were already provided.

These people truly embraced what it means to love your neighbor and show hospitality. I honestly didn't know how to respond to their kindness because up till that point I had never been on a church staff and had never been welcomed to a new place like this before. But, I graciously accepted and knew I was really going to love working at this church.

In the four jobs I have had since graduating from seminary, I have been welcomed with open arms at each one involving my own unloading team, meals for a week, cards, welcome banners, welcome receptions, decorated office, and even a team of men who helped prepare a cabin with insulation so that my family could live there temporarily during the coldest winter ever.

But, I'm here to tell you that you don't have to have a host of people waiting to welcome you to know this is God's calling for you in this season of life. Just look at Abram. There is no mention in Genesis 12 of people lined up at their house eagerly waiting for them with bread, meat and wine. No one was there to help them unload all their possessions and help them set up their new residence. No one. Not one single person is mentioned. Of course, no one knew they were coming, even Abram didn't know where he was going. How could he let anyone know he was coming if he didn't even know where his journey would take him?

When God calls you to move to a new place, He is taking care of every single detail. Maybe you'll be welcomed with a huge party with streamers, balloons, and cake. But, maybe you'll only be welcomed with a sign hanging above your office door on your first day. No matter what kind of welcome you receive, be confident in the calling God has given you and never doubt. God is going to use you despite the circumstances or welcome you receive at this new ministry.

### Remembering the Lord

When Abram and his family arrived in the land of Canaan, it says they traveled through the land, stopping at several different spots along the way. At each spot, God spoke to Abram and afterward Abram built an altar to the Lord (Genesis 12:6-9).

All throughout the Old Testament we find where God has spoken to people and then they build an altar. Abram is just one of these people. Building altars was a way of remembering what God spoke to them or what He did for them (remember Samuel's altar I mentioned in chapter one?). God wanted all His people to remember the things He had done for them at each place.

In this example in Genesis 12, God told Abram he would give his offspring this land (Genesis 12:7). God promises Abram this land for his descendants. And we all know that He sure does follow through on this promise.

At each stage in our journey of following God, I think God also wants us to remember Him. You may be called to move every few years, or you may be called to move only a few times in your life, or maybe only once. But no matter how many times you move, I believe it's important to reflect and remember the work God has done through you in that city.

I like to remember by writing it down. I make notes or write stories about the things God has done in that place. I don't ever want to forget the mighty ways God has worked through me. My memory is not as good as it once was (I blame that on childbirth...I am convinced I lost memory cells once I had babies). I can't rely on my memory so that's why I make sure to write down the things I don't want to forget. And then I praise God for how He used me in that place. This is my way of building an altar for the Lord.

Before moving on to that next ministry or calling, reflect and remember on how God has been with you, how God has used you, and how God's power and love was spread to so many people. God impresses on us the importance of remembering because that helps us to remember how faithful He is to us and will always be with us.

### Finding Freedom

My freedom from the fear of moving was made known to me through the story of Abram. And, within this fear of moving were multiple other fears. I feared the actual call to move and I feared that I wouldn't be able to obey God without doubting. I had fear of God not blessing me, the fear of having to give up everything, the fear of my family not supporting me, and the fear of not being welcomed. That's a lot of fears springing up from one main fear.

I am so thankful God also showed me that it's important to remember Him. I believe the remembrance of all He has done for us in each stage is what breaks off each little tiny fear and completely severs the overall fear of moving. What joy and peace God brings to us when we can see past the fear of moving and remember His faithfulness in every place He calls.

If you have been afraid of moving to a new place or you have recently moved and just aren't sure of your call, get out a journal and a pen...and start remembering. Fill those pages with the goodness of the Lord. See the many blessings He has provided for you along the way. Build your altars before the Lord. Remember God's love for you and how He has always provided for you. Then you will begin to see the fear of moving fade away and be replaced with a sense of peace, excitement, and hopefulness at all God will do through you in this new phase of His calling. And you will be able to sing this hymn to a glorious and faithful God:

*"Great is thy faithfulness! Great is thy faithfulness! Morning by morning new mercies I see. All I have needed thy hand hath provided; Great is thy faithfulness, Lord unto me!"*[4]

### Rise Up Prayer

*All Knowing Father, we thank You for where we are right now, the place in which You are using us in this very moment. Perhaps there are some of us who sense You calling us to a new place. This terrifies us and it causes us to freeze and not want to move because of this fear. We boldly ask You to rise up, O Lord. Defrost our fear of moving so we can move forward to the new place You are calling us. Help us to let go and trust You with all we have, not relying on our own understanding, but acknowledging You as our Great Provider. In Jesus' name, Amen.*

---

4   Thomas Chisholm, "Great is Thy Faithfulness", 1925

# DID YOU SAY SOMETHING?
## *Fear of No One Listening*

*G*od must really have a good sense of humor! He's got *to be kidding! There's no way God can be serious about what He just said!*

God had just asked Moses to go to Egypt, talk to Pharaoh and tell him to set the Israelites free. He saw several problems with this request from God. Moses could not speak very well. He stuttered and stammered and had trouble getting words out sometimes. He was not eloquent enough in his speech to even begin to speak to someone as powerful as Pharaoh. He also feared being the laughing stock of Egypt. Pharaoh and his officials would for sure spread the word that some crazy old man who couldn't even speak well, tried to convince him to let go of his slaves. And then, who was he to be the one to go? He was not famous. He did not have power. He was a nobody…just an old man tending to his father-in-law's sheep. Nothing special about him.

How was he going to convince the Lord he was not the man for the job? Would God listen to him and see that He had made a mistake? Would He realize He picked the wrong man? Didn't God know that no one would listen to him?

### Be Still and Listen

Have you ever gotten that call from God before? You know...the one to be still and listen before Him? If you have, then you know how extremely hard that is. To truly give time to just be still and listen to the Lord is not an easy task.

God called me to this stillness and listening in October 2014. I wanted to be obedient to Him, but how was I going to do this and where do I even start?

God led me to a book called, *Enjoy the Silence: A 30-Day Experiment in Listening to God* by Maggie and Duffy Robbins. For thirty days, the Robbins guide you through Scripture, giving you questions and thoughts to ponder as you are still and as you listen to the Lord. I kept a journal of my thoughts and how I felt God was speaking to me during those thirty days. It was an amazing month of listening and I was so thankful to have done it.

As I began to think about this chapter in my book and what I would write, God guided me back to the journal I kept in those thirty days and He specifically led me to day twenty-four. On this day, the Scripture was Psalm 40. In this chapter, David is crying out to God as he feels like he's in a dark, deep pit. While in this pit, the Lord heard his cry and lifted him out and set his feet upon a rock. It's a great chapter of God's faithfulness to David and how David remembers that and proclaims this aloud.

On this day, one of the questions posed by the authors for reflection was: *"What is it in your life that makes your pit so deep and discouraging?"*[5]

On that day, I am blown away by what I wrote because it has to do directly with what this chapter is about. I love how God can bring you back to things you wrote when you need to hear it the most.

In my journal I wrote that I felt my pit was called "The Pit of No One Listening". During that time in 2014, I was struggling with a few things related to that. God had laid on my heart just the year before the call to write and speak. I had started a blog and was being faithful to the call to write, or at least I thought I was. Then in early 2014, I felt God calling me to write my story; to write a book about my fears of serving Him in the ministry and also to speak and share this with others. And as exciting as this all sounds, it's also very frightening. *Why me, Lord?*

On day twenty-four, I journaled about this calling and why anyone would listen to me speak or listen to the words I write in a book. First of all, I was feeling frustrated in my personal life. I love my kids and they are the joys of my life,

---

5 Maggie Robbins and Duffy Robbins, *Enjoy the Silence: A 30-Day Experiment in Listening to God* (Grand Rapids: Zondervan, 2005), 99

but they don't always listen. I ask them to do something and they act like they don't even hear me speak. And if they did hear me say it, then they question the things I ask of them. If you are a parent then you probably understand this frustration. Why can't they just say, "Yes ma'am" and then do it? Why totally ignore me and do the opposite of what I ask?

Then there are times when my spouse is distracted when I am trying to ask him or tell him something. It usually involves a sport on TV, which is fine, but sometimes I wish he would turn it off so I wouldn't have to repeat myself several times.

Then there are the kids at church. I love them so much and they are a joy in my life, too. But, we all know kids love to talk and getting them to sit still is hard at times. And getting them to listen is a difficult task, too. Sometimes I feel like I'm there just talking to myself. Do they hear the Bible story I am teaching them? Do they truly get what Jesus did for them? Are they understanding the Bible and how I am teaching them? There are days when I think they don't…days when I feel like giving up. Why bother when no one is listening?

When God called me to write and speak, I questioned the call. Why do I need to do this, Lord? No one is going to listen. And why would they? I talk super-fast and get extremely nervous when I speak in front of a crowd. Who am I to even attempt to write a blog, a book, or even speak to large groups of people? Why would they care to hear from Vanessa Myers?

### *Moses' List of Reasons*

All these questions I had for God made me think of Moses and how he had some of these same questions. The things he said to God are very similar to my fear in doing this whole writing/speaking thing.

Moses didn't think the Israelites would even listen to him, much less believe him when he said God appeared to him (Exodus 4:1). Maybe he thinks they will call him crazy. Or perhaps they really won't even care about anything he says because who is he to tell them anything about God? But God provides him with a few different visuals for the Israelites in case they wouldn't believe (a staff that turns into a snake, a hand inside a cloak that turns leprous, the Nile River water that turns into blood). God is so good like that.

> "But Moses said to the Lord, 'O my Lord, I have never been eloquent, neither in the past nor even now that you have spoken to your servant; but I am slow of speech and slow of tongue'" (Exodus 4:10).

And here's when I want to scream out, "Yes, Lord, here's what I'm talking about!" I am not eloquent. I'm just a southern girl from the state of Georgia. I don't talk in fancy words and can't pray lofty prayers. Everything about me is simple; from my speech to my writing to the way I dress to the way I act even to the things I cook. I'm a simple kind of girl. So, God, why would anyone want to listen to that kind of person?

Moses had a speech impediment; one that caused him to stutter and be slow to speak. It was hard to understand him. So how in the world was he going to speak to someone as mighty as Pharaoh and then also to thousands of people about following God and getting out of Egypt? Well, there was only one way he was going to do that…with the help of the Lord.

God immediately speaks to him again with these words:

> "Who gives speech to mortals? Who makes them mute or deaf, seeing or blind? Is it not I, the Lord? Now go, and I will be with your mouth and teach you what you are to speak" (Exodus 4:11-12).

Did you get that? God told Moses he was going to be with him and teach him what to speak. Moses wasn't going to have to worry about the words he would be saying to the very powerful Pharaoh. God explicitly told him so. But, it seems that our good friend Moses just didn't get it. He's afraid and he doubted his abilities too much. His next words to God are:

> "O my Lord, please send someone else" (Exodus 4:13).

Did you cringe a little when you read that? Almost like you are embarrassed for Moses? *Why did you say that, Moses? Don't you know God doesn't want anybody else? He wants you. He wouldn't have called you if He didn't want you for this assignment. He chose you. Only you. He will teach you what you are to say. No worries, Moses. You got this.*

Of course, we know Moses shouldn't have said that to God. And God was angry with him. So, God had to throw in some help for him in the form of his brother, Aaron. But God still used Moses to be the leader for His people.

### Finding Freedom

Here's what I want to focus on in this passage in Exodus…Moses was afraid that no one would listen to him. That's exactly how I have felt at times during my years since I was first called into the ministry. And that's especially been true for me since He called me to write and speak in 2013.

God has been so gracious and has shown me how to overcome this fear by doing three simple things. These things I have read about many times before in one of the most read chapters in the Bible: faith, hope, and love. But I'm going to start at the end because, as the Bible says, "the greatest of these is love" (1 Corinthians 13:13).

### Love

"If I speak in the tongues of mortals and of angels, but do not have love, I am a noisy gong or a clanging cymbal" (1 Corinthians 13:1).

That one verse sums it all up for me. I can speak and write and share the message of God with many others, but if I don't have love then I will sound like an instrument that is annoying and hurts my ears. Words will be coming out and I may be talking about how awesome God is, but if I don't have love...that true love of Christ...then no one is going to pay a bit of attention to what I am saying.

Now you may be saying, *"Well, Vanessa, if you are speaking about God then surely you love Him, otherwise you wouldn't speak about Him."* And you are right...to a point.

I have loved God my whole life. I was raised in the church, accepted Jesus as my Savior as a child, went to seminary to learn more about Him, and have been serving in the local church for the past seventeen years. But it hasn't been till these past four years that I have had this strong desire to know God, to really love God with every inch of my being. It's a love that is hard to describe, but it consumes me. It's this kind of desire where I want nothing more than to sit in His Presence, read my Bible, sing loudly to the praise songs on my phone, and raise my hands as I worship Him. I honestly and truly find myself loving God with my whole heart.

Beth Moore has written a book called *Audacious*. In this book she describes the difference between needing God and wanting God. We all know we need to love God and we do that, but the difference comes when we move from needing to love God to wanting to love God.

Beth says:

*"We will never love Him just because we need to. We will only love Him audaciously because we want to."*[6]

Isn't this so true? When we move past our need and realize we want to love Jesus so boldly, then that's when our lives are changed. That's when we can let go of this fear that no one is going to listen to us speak about God. I can guarantee you that if you love God with a boldness that you can't even talk about without crying, then you can bet that people will hear you and will listen to you. They will see your true love for the Lord and will desire to have that love for God, too.

Love God boldly. Love Him with every inch of your being. Love Him fully. When you do, you will be able to do great things because of your love for Him.

### Hope

Hope is defined as "to want something to happen or be true and think that it could happen and be true."[7] We can hope that a lot of things will happen for us: good health, financial stability, true love, happiness, job promotion, to be blessed with material things, to have many friends, to be successful. So many areas in our life where we have hope.

---

6   Beth Moore, *Audacious* (Nashville: B & H Publishing Group, 2015), 92

7   "hope." Merriam-Webster.com. 2016. http://www.merriam-webster.com (June 27, 2016)

But the question we have to ask ourselves when we are being fearful of no one listening is this: What is my hope built on?

Is my hope built on my own abilities? Is my hope built on outcomes? Is my hope built on my own success? I can tell you for sure, that if you have built your hope on anything other than Jesus Christ, your fear of no one listening to you will never go away.

Who wants to listen to someone who thinks they are superior? Who wants to listen to someone who thinks their words are their own? Who wants to listen to someone whose hope is not in Jesus Christ?

I love the hymn *My Hope is Built* and in the first verse it says:

*"My hope is built on nothing less than Jesus' blood and righteousness."* [8]

I have come to the realization that my hope has to be built only on Jesus. It has to be Him and Him alone. I can't hope in my own self. I can't hope that my own sermons, talks, workshops, blog posts, or books will be heard and received well. I can't hope that anyone will listen to me just because I am Vanessa Myers. My hope has to be built on Jesus. It's only because of Him that I can speak, write, or talk about Him. He gives all of us gifts to use so we will be able to serve Him. When we use those gifts with our

---

8   Edward Mote, "My Hope is Built on Nothing Less", 1837

hope built on Him, then others will hear and they will listen.

I believe our fears are strong when we don't have our hope built on Him and Him alone. Satan convinces us there is no hope in God Almighty. He tricks us into thinking we don't need God and that causes us to lose our hope. Without our hope in Jesus then we cannot speak about Him. We will lose that love, desire and passion for Him. We replace all those with our fears. We will stop speaking about God and sharing His love for others. And that's exactly what Satan wants.

In order to get past this fear of no one listening, then we must stand firm in our hope in Jesus Christ. Don't get caught standing on the sand. That's when we start sinking. That's where Satan wants us. We must find our way back to the solid rock…getting back to that hope in Jesus Christ. Then when we speak about Him, we will not sink, but we will be heard and His love will spread over all the earth. He is our firm foundation and He is the only true way to eternal life.

### Faith

There is one final component in squashing this fear you have of no one listening to you speak about Jesus. And that is faith. I'm not just talking about a tiny amount of faith…not just enough faith to get you through this calling. I'm talking about a bold kind of faith. A faith that does not waver. A faith that is strong. A faith that is willing to be obedient to all God asks.

That kind of faith is not easy, either. That's why it's important to have that passionate and infinite love for the Lord. And it's why you need a strong love and a firm hope in Jesus Christ. Without these two your faith would be nothing. You wouldn't be able to go out and speak boldly about Him. You wouldn't step out and speak for the Lord if you didn't love Him wholeheartedly and have your hope in Him. You need love and hope in order to have a faith that lives boldly for the Lord.

My question for you is…Are you willing?

Do you truly want to speak to others about God? Do you WANT to love Him? Do you WANT to have your hope in Him? Do you WANT to have a faith that will walk on water?

When you can answer yes to these questions, then your fear of no one listening to you will be gone. You will speak so boldly for the Lord that ears will hear. People will see God through you. People will desire to have the love for God that they see in you. People will listen.

Take some time to pray through this. If you desire to speak for the Lord, then know He will go before you and you have nothing to fear. Ask God to give you an extravagant love for Him, a hope that is built on Him, and a faith that will boldly go and is obedient to Him. When you do this, your fear will sink so quickly and your feet will be standing on the rock that is solid and cannot be moved.

### Rise Up Prayer

*Almighty God, we have learned that living a life for You is hard. And when You call us to share Your love with others we become afraid to do that because we feel insufficient in our calling. We believe no one will listen because we aren't important enough, or like Moses, we just don't have eloquent speech. Rise up, O Lord and free us from this sinking sand of fear. Set our feet back on the Rock, Jesus Christ. Show us that others will listen when we have strong love, hope, and faith built in You. Give us the confidence we need to speak freely and boldly about You. In Jesus' name, Amen.*

# 10

# I MUST SUCCEED
## *Fear of Failure*

*Peter, Peter what are you doing, following that man? You gave up your life of fishing, will it really last? Think about the way things might have been if you'd remained at sea. You'd still be a fisherman. Peter, you're such a fool.*

*Peter, Peter what are you doing, sinking in the waves? You thought you could walk on water, but now you're sinking down. Think about the way things might have been if you'd remained at sea. You'd still be a fisherman. Peter, you're such a fool.*

*Peter, Peter what are you doing, crying by the fire? You told them that you did not know Him but now He's gone and died. Think about the way things might have been if you'd remained at sea. You'd still be a fisherman. Peter, you're such a fool.*

*Peter, Peter what are you doing, hanging upside down?*
*Peter you know you're dying…dying for your Lord. Think*
*about the way things might have been if you'd remained at*
*sea. You'd still be a fisherman. Peter, you're such a fool.*
*Oh how I long to be such a fool…* [9]

Peter was a failure. He couldn't believe he let his Lord
down. There had been times when he didn't believe what
Jesus was saying to him. Why had he been so blind to see
who Jesus was at times?

Then there was the time when he saw Jesus walking
to their boat on the water. He couldn't believe his eyes,
but Jesus really was doing something nobody else could
do…He was walking on water. Peter got excited and asked
Jesus to call for him to come to Him if it was really Him.
So Jesus called out to him to come meet Him and he
began to walk on water. He, Peter the disciple, was doing
something Jesus was doing. He was walking on water, too!
How cool!! But then he failed Jesus. He began to doubt.
And down he went. Sinking in the waves. He had lost his
faith.

Maybe the worst of all failures was when he denied
knowing Christ three times…just as Jesus said he would.
Why would he say he didn't know Jesus? He loved Jesus.
He had been with Him for three years and had seen Him
perform some mighty miracles and heal many people. But

---

9 Anonymous folk song about the life of Peter, the disciple of Jesus; sung
by Camp Glisson staff in 1999; https://www.youtube.com/watch?v=97_
fDhu9fxo

yet, when it came down to it, he denied Christ. He denied even knowing who He was. He was so ashamed.

He had failed Jesus. And he wept.

### Being Successful

I like to succeed.

But, lurking right behind the need to succeed is the fear of failure. And I don't like to fail. It's not something I like to talk about either. I wish I didn't have to tell you I have this fear. Why? Because I don't like people thinking that I don't have it all together or I can't do everything. Like I said, I like to succeed at everything I do.

This need to succeed and fear of failure became very clear while reading a book called *I Know His Name: Discovering Power in the Names of God,* by Wendy Blight. In the first chapter she asks, *"What good gifts from God do you desire more than the Giver?"*[10]

As I prayed about the answer to this question, God brought to light that I desire success more than I desire Him. *Really, God? I do?* How could I be more concerned with success when what I was striving to do was for Him?

And then shame hit me like a ton of bricks. I *was* doing that. I did not like to think I was putting success before Him. But truth be told, I was.

I believe I put success before God because I have this huge fear of failure. And for me, this fear of failure really

---

10 Wendy Blight, *I Know His Name: Discovering Power in the Names of God* (Nashville: Thomas Nelson, 2015), 19

translates into a fear of failing and disappointing others. I seem to have a history of this fear, too. It stretches all the way back to middle school.

Grades were pretty important to me as a kid. I had to make A's and B's. Not because my mom told me I had to (although she did expect me to try my best), but really because I wanted to. And that want came from a desire to succeed.

In 6th grade I got a C on my report card in Language Arts. I was so scared to show my mom because I knew I would get in trouble for it. She knew what my capability was, and I was not a C student. I made A's and B's. So this C, to me, meant failure. I had failed at being a good student.

I came home that afternoon terrified. My stomach was in knots. I needed to tell my mom, but I was too afraid. So, I did what any great kid would do…I wrote her a note. I left my report card and this beautifully crafted note of apology on her nightstand. She wouldn't see it till after I went to sleep and there was no way she would wake her sleeping child to yell at her.

Well, I was wrong.

The lights came on in my dark room while I was getting my beauty sleep and then the yelling commenced. I got a punishment that probably no other kid got…ever. I was grounded from the TV for the next six weeks until the next report card came out and I could show I raised my grade in Language Arts. That was the longest six weeks of my life. No TV for an 11-year old was devastating, especially when my two sisters could watch it. It was torture! Pure torture.

Why such a harsh punishment? Well, I think it was because my mother knew I could do better than a C and she saw that the TV was a huge distraction for me. It kept me from studying and doing well in school. She knew what I was capable of doing and she pushed me to do my best. And you better believe I worked hard over the course of those six weeks. I wasn't going to fail or disappoint myself or my mother again. And of course I got my grade up to an A.

My fear of failure as a kid had to do with disappointing my mother. I did not want to let her down by making bad grades. She knew I was a smart girl and I could work harder and do better than a C. I worked so hard to not fail as a student (or make less than a B) and when I got a C that year it was devastating (at the time).

### *Ministry Failures*

The fear of failure has spilled over into my professional life as a full-time ministry leader. How could you be afraid of failing when you serve God, you ask? I know it's a crazy fear, but it's very much alive in many people in the ministry. And I am one of those.

What does fear of failure look like when you work in the church? For me, failure is calculated in several ways. If I have low numbers in my ministry then I am a failure. Here's the ministry equation: more people + more people = a successful ministry. If I don't have a thriving ministry then I could be fired. Now, that's me talking. No pastor has ever told me I would be fired if I didn't have a certain number of kids or teens in my ministry at church. But, how can I look at my ministry and consider myself a success if I don't have very many people in it?

Have you ever thought this...if I don't have big numbers in my ministry, then I am not bringing enough families into the church and I am not affecting their kids and leading them to Jesus? At times during my years in the ministry, I have thought this. I must be doing something wrong because if more people are not coming to our church, that means the knowledge of Jesus is not getting spread, which means I am a failure.

In my seventeen years of ministry, I have only had one pastor who was concerned about numbers. And God bless him. It was only because he was under a lot of pressure to grow the church, too. It's tough when you've got people breathing down your neck expecting you to do great things and bring in a lot of people into the church. And when you don't then well, you get the boot. Again, no one has done this to me, but it's just the fear of failure I feel as a ministry leader. Which, is one of the reasons I strive so hard to be successful in the ministry. And one of the reasons God has shown me that I am putting success before Him.

Another ministry failure is lack of support. This could mean no support from your senior pastor, no support from the parents in your ministry, and nobody volunteering to serve in your ministry. When you're a loner in the church as a staff member, then it's not a good situation. As I mentioned in chapter three, ministry can be lonely, but you definitely do not want the loneliness to come because no one supports you. If you don't have the support of your senior pastor, parents, and church members then you are a complete failure. Right? No, that's not always the case.

Another big ministry failure I have put on myself is that if I can't count the number of kids who have accepted Jesus as their Savior, then I am a big, fat failure. I have heard so many children's ministers rave about the number of kids who have been saved in their ministry. And then I look at myself and wonder if the kids in our ministry have done that. I know that there are (two of them being my daughters), but I think that since I don't keep count then I am a failure. Maybe I should do that. Will that mean I am more successful and won't be such a failure?

When I was in college I went on a mission trip to Clearwater, Florida with the Baptist Student Union. One of our roles that week was to pass out tracts and talk to people on the beach about Jesus. Each night we would gather back together and talk about our day. Sitting in those meetings I can remember feeling like a failure. So many people shared how they led people to Christ that day on the beach. And me? Well, all I could think was that I must not have been doing God's work that day because I didn't lead anyone in a salvation prayer.

Over the years since then, God has shown me that success doesn't come in numbers. Success comes when I follow the Lord. If I am spreading the name of Jesus and sharing His love with others, then I am doing what He wants. He will take the seeds I have planted and make them grow in the hearts of those I speak with. I don't have to have a long list of the number of salvations I did while I was in the ministry. I just need to be faithful and share Him.

For all of these ministry failures I have, do you think that God is disappointed in me if I don't succeed at everything He asks me to do? The number one thing I do not want to do is disappoint God. I can't stand the thought of God looking at me and seeing me as a failure; someone who doesn't quite have it all together, someone who did not put her trust in Him, someone who for the life of her could not seem to have enough faith in God for the task at hand. I do not want to fail God.

*Am I the only person who fears failure and disappointing God?*

By no means.

The Bible is full of people who not only feared failure, but actually (by any objective standard) failed. Let's take a look at a couple of them.

### Failures in the Bible

The first people that come to mind for me that failed God are the Israelites. And they didn't just fail one time. They failed many times. They were excited to be free from slavery from the Egyptians. God had delivered them. He was going to take care of them because they were His people. They probably thought this was going to be an easy ride and nothing bad would happen.

But, as we all know, it was not an easy road. And God never said it would be. He freed them and was ready to take them on to the Promised Land. However, that didn't happen for forty years. They grumbled and complained, hardened their hearts, were angry and upset, were impatient, did not listen to God, and flat out did the exact opposite of what He asked of them.

They failed. And they had disappointed God. But did God ever leave them? Not for a second. Did God stop loving them? Not at all. Did God turn His back on them because they failed? Never.

Peter is another example of someone who failed several times. The first one comes in Matthew 14 when Jesus walks on water. The disciples are a little freaked out when they see a man walking on the water toward their boat. They actually thought it was a ghost and cried out in fear. Jesus responds by telling them not to be afraid.

Then Peter gets pretty brave. He says:

"Lord, if it is you, command me to come to you on the water" (Matthew 14:28).

And guess what happens? Peter walks on the water toward Jesus. He's doing it. Not afraid at all. He's probably thinking this is pretty cool. But then his humanness kicks in and he starts to remember people can't walk on water. And Peter does the worse thing possible…he begins to doubt. That's when he sinks. And that's when Jesus says:

"You of little faith, why did you doubt?" (Matthew 14:31b).

What a stab to the heart, don't you think? Jesus told Peter he had little faith. Peter had failed because of his lack of faith. The Bible doesn't go on to say anything about Peter's response to this, but, you know it had to cut deep. I am sure Peter was embarrassed, ashamed, and completely sorry about his lack of faith. He had doubted Jesus and had lost his faith for a split second.

Did Jesus kick him off His team? No. Did Jesus stop loving him? Not at all. Did his doubting keep Jesus from using him to serve Him? No way.

### *Finding Freedom*

Looking at these examples from the Bible brings me comfort and hope. They help me realize that other people have failed; people God and Jesus loved dearly. And what did God and Jesus do? They remained faithful and always kept their promises despite the shortcomings and failures of the Israelites and Peter.

In finding freedom from my fear of failure, God has helped me to realize a few things: I will fail, Jesus never fails, and my anchor must be deep.

First of all, I must to come to terms with the fact that I will fail. Yes, the woman who wants to succeed at everything will fail. The woman who is a people pleaser will fail. The woman who wants to be perfect will fail. The woman who despises disappointing others, especially God, will fail. It's inevitable. I am a human being and am not capable of being perfect. I love this verse that reminds me of my shortcomings:

> "My flesh and my heart may fail, but God is the strength of my heart and my portion forever" (Psalm 73:26).

God reminds us in this verse that we are going to fail. Our flesh and our hearts are not destined to be flawless. We are sinners who are in need of God's redemption and grace. I am so thankful for this verse because it helps lift a weight off of my shoulders. It reminds me that God is my strength and I should not be relying on myself. I am to depend solely on God and His strength. He is all I need.

Second, I am reminded that Jesus never fails. Yes, I will fail, but Jesus never will. Doesn't that bring you such peace and comfort? This should erase every ounce of fear you have and replace it with the utmost confidence in our God who will never fail. Not in a God that may sometimes fail, but we have faith in our God who will NEVER fail.

My grandmother had a plaque hanging in her house above the door to her kitchen that said, "Jesus never fails." I always loved that sign as a child and believed it, but it takes on a whole different level of meaning for me now. I have lived through fear of failing and when I look at this sign now I am can honestly say 100% that my Jesus does not fail. This sign hangs in my mother's house now and maybe one day I will have the honor of hanging it in my house. I love visual reminders of God's unending faithfulness to us.

Third, my anchor of faith must be deep. How deep is your anchor? Does it reach all the way down and firmly hold when stormy weather comes? Or is it barely in the water, unable to find anything stable? If we want to overcome our fear of failure, we must have our anchors of faith planted firmly in the One who can give us living water. We will keep failing over and over if we don't have faith that runs deep and wide. When the fears of failure come crashing in on us, we need to make sure our anchors are secure and we need to hang on because Satan wants to rip that anchor up and keep us away from believing that God is with us.

We can have deep anchors of faith by spending time in His Word. Soak in every single piece of Scripture. Write it down. Memorize it. Hang it where you will be reminded of it. Share it with your children. Scripture is our best defense against the enemy. We can also have deep anchors of faith by remembering God's faithfulness. God instructed Moses to write down the ways in which He was faithful. One example is from when the Israelites battled the Amalekites and won. God used the prayers of Moses, his staff, and his friends as a support to conquer the evil Amalekites. Exodus 17:14 says,

"Then the Lord said to Moses: 'Write this as a reminder in a book and recite it in the hearing of

Joshua: I will utterly blot out the remembrance of Amalek from under heaven.'"

God wanted the Israelites to remember how faithful He was when He conquered the Amalekites. So the next time a big giant came along and they were scared of failing and they were not being confident in God, they could look back on this glorious battle and remember God would be with them and He would not fail.

Do you have a journal where you can write down God's faithfulness? If not, go get one. And keep up with it. You should be able to fill it up quickly. Write down your fears of failure. What are you afraid of failing at? What keeps you from succeeding? How does God work through your failures and your successes? You will be so thankful you can go back and remember how God brought you through your failures in spite of your flaws. How God used your failures for good. How God never left your side.

My ministry outlook has changed tremendously since I have dealt with my fear of failure. Recognizing that I will fail and yet Jesus never fails has been the key to letting go of this fear. This recognition has opened my eyes to seeing I cannot put success before God. I cannot be afraid to fail because, truth be told, I will.

Low numbers does not equal failure. I have learned if I am ministering to one person, then I am doing what God wants me to do. If what I do for Him affects just one person then I am not a failure. And believe me when I say this is true.

Lack of support does not mean I am a failure. Yes, it hurts, but I have learned that if I am doing God's will, then I will always have the best supporter on my team, Jesus Christ. If you do find yourself feeling like you don't have support, then start praying. Pray that God will remind you of Him and how He is your #1 supporter. Ask God to open up doors of trust between your boss, your parents, your friends, or volunteers. Pray that God will provide you with a support team.

Not knowing how many kids I have led to Christ does not mean I am a failure. I see myself as a seed planter. I am planting the seed of faith into these children. Someone else may water it and God will grow that seed of faith in a person. Like Paul says,

> "I planted, Apollos watered, but God gave the growth. So neither the one who plants nor the one who waters is anything, but only God who gives the growth. The one who plants and the one who waters have a common purpose, and each will receive wages according to the labor of each. For we are God's servants, working together; you are God's field, God's building" (1 Corinthians 3:6-9).

It doesn't matter if one hundred kids get saved at your church service, or just one. God is the one who brings growth to the seeds you plant. You are not a failure for only seeing one person give their life to Christ. Again, if you are doing God's will and planting seeds, God will take care of the growth.

I want to leave you with a Scripture verse. This is a verse I believe will help you remember to put God first in all you do as well as to help you let go of your fear of failure and to put your trust in Him.

"Not to us, O Lord, not to us, but to your name give glory, for the sake of your steadfast love and your faithfulness" (Psalm 115:1).

Always give God the glory. When you do this, you will not fear failing anymore because you know that Jesus never fails.

### Rise Up Prayer

*Everlasting Father, You know that we aren't perfect. You know that we are only human and we are not without sin. You know there are times when we will fail. But this fear of failure causes great stress in many of us. We want to please You, we want to succeed, and we want to be the best at all You have called us to do. But we ask now, Lord, for You to rise up. Free our minds from thinking we are complete failures when we don't succeed. Remind us You are the Almighty God and Your love never fails. Remind us Your grace, mercy, and forgiveness is all we need when sin gets the best of us. Help us to have deep anchors of faith in You so that when the enemy comes with his lies that we are failures, we won't go astray and forget You and all You have called us to do. In Jesus' name we pray, Amen.*

## 11

# EXCUSES, EXCUSES
### *Fear of Giving Up*

Was Mordecai serious? Did he realize that what he just asked of her could get her killed? What was he thinking, asking her to do something like this?

Mordecai had just asked Esther to save the Jews by going to see the king without having been invited. I mean…that's such an insane request! People get killed for stuff like this. Just because she was the queen didn't mean she could ask whatever she wanted of the king.

But she did love her people, the Jews. How could she just sit by and watch them all be killed? If she did nothing and they all died, then she would be deeply saddened. Her cousin, Mordecai, who was like a father to her, would die as well. Could she really just sit by and do nothing?

However, she was terrified. She didn't want to be killed, either. Her list of excuses seemed to be growing. All she wanted to do was give up and hope the king would change his mind. What should she do?

### *My List of Excuses*

What if I told you that I have never given excuses to God before? Would you believe me? I hope you wouldn't because that statement would be a big fat lie.

Sometimes I feel like I am the *queen* of excuses when it comes to God. When I feel God speaking to me, my mouth spews forth a long list of excuses of why I could never do what He is asking. I don't even give God a chance to finish speaking when the excuses start forming in my head. And to me they are pretty good excuses. Most of these excuses have to deal with the fears I have been writing about in this book:

- You've got the wrong person for the job, Lord.
- I don't need to learn anything else, Lord.
- I don't want to be alone, Lord.
- You know I don't handle change very well, Lord.
- People will not like me and they will criticize what I do, Lord.
- I am afraid of my boss, Lord.
- I am not good enough to do that, Lord.
- I hate moving, Lord.
- Nobody even knows who I am so they aren't going to listen to me, Lord.
- I will fail at this, Lord.
- I can pretty much promise I will give up, Lord.

Sometimes I make it past these excuses and fears and actually do what God wants me to do. I feel confident, bold, and passionate about serving Him. It's amazing to obey God and see the many ways He blesses you through your obedience.

But, then I stop dead in my tracks. I don't seem to be moving forward at all. It's like something is blocking my way and I just can't keep going. *What is this, Lord?*

Well, it seems I have stumbled upon an old friend of mine. We go way back. I've seen him before, but I'm not too happy to see him now. I thought I had gotten rid of this friend but it looks like he's trying to make an appearance in my life again. Maybe he thinks he will win this time.

This old friend is called "giving up." When God calls me to something, I don't want to see this old friend. He is not a good one to have. But, somehow I seem to allow him to worm his way back into my life, even when I don't want him. This fear of giving up also seems to creep in after I do what God has called me to do. And this fear brings up a whole new list of excuses:

- I'm too tired, Lord.
- It's been too hard, Lord.
- I don't really need to do this anymore, Lord.
- I just don't want to do it anymore, Lord.
- I am not getting anything out of this, Lord.
- What's the point in doing this anymore, Lord?
- I'm not cut out for this, Lord.
- I'm too old for this, Lord.

- I'm too overwhelmed, Lord.
- The demands are endless, Lord.
- I don't have any support, Lord.
- Where are you in all this, Lord?

The excuses seem to pile up right before me, stretching much taller than me and making me not be able to see God and the task He has for me. I have lost my focus and I have lost sight of God. When that happens, well, I might as well just give up, right? Looks like God might have left me anyways, so I'm just going to go ahead and throw in the towel on this calling from God. No sense in doing it anymore.

I cringe while I am typing this. It's painful to write what I have felt so many times. How do I get to the point where I don't want to do God's will anymore? How do I let myself be stopped by this fear of giving up? How do I possibly want to give up on this calling? Don't I know that God has great plans for me? I must keep going, but I just want to give up.

### I'm Not Giving Up

Giving up has turned into a fear of mine. I have seen myself ready and willing to step out and serve God. So I gather up the courage and walk down this new path and begin doing it, but then I turn back because of excuses. Lame ones at that.

I don't want to be that woman anymore. I don't want to be a woman who gives up on the Lord because it's too hard, or I'm tired, or I am overwhelmed. I want to live a life boldly for the Lord, not believing that I will give up on the task He has for me just because I have a history of giving up. No, I am going to conquer this fear. I may have to face off with it every time I get a call from God, but I believe I can conquer this fear and will not give up.

### Esther is My Role Model

Esther is one of my favorite people in the Bible. I love her story and am inspired by it. I believe Esther can teach us so much about not giving up when God calls us.

Esther was a Jew living in a kingdom under King Xerxes reign. She was an orphan who was adopted by her cousin Mordecai. Time came for a new queen to be picked for the king and Esther was the one who found favor with him and she was chosen as the new queen.

Life as queen seemed to be going well for Esther for about four years. And then she was faced with a huge crisis. Haman, the king's right hand man, was infuriated when he saw that Mordecai was not willing to bow down to him. Mordecai refused to do this because he was a Jew. This ticked Haman off and so he plotted to kill all the Jews in the Persian Empire. So, Haman told the king that there were certain people in his kingdom who did not follow all of the king's laws. He convinced the king to sign into law the destruction of these people. And Haman said he would pay ten thousand talents of silver into the king's treasuries for their destruction. With no questions asked, King Xerxes signed this decree and sent it out. He sealed it with his signet ring, which we find out later, is unbreakable. Any decree signed by the king with this ring cannot be broken or overturned.

When Mordecai learns of this new decree, he is extremely upset. Scripture says he "tore his clothes and put on sackcloth and ashes and went through the city, wailing with a loud and bitter cry" (Esther 4:1). Esther hears from her maids about the condition of Mordecai and asks one of her servants to go find out what is wrong with him. Mordecai tells the servant about the new decree and how Esther and her people (the Jews) will soon be destroyed. He pleads with Esther to go to the king and stand up for her people.

When her servant reports back to her, Esther is upset, too. And then she begins to list off her excuses of not doing what Mordecai has asked of her, which I believe is what God is asking her to do, too. Her excuses include (Esther 4:10-11):

- The king has not called me to come in to see him for thirty days.
- If I approach him without being called I could be put to death.

What she's probably also subtlety saying here in her excuses is:
- You're asking too much of me.
- I am afraid.
- I don't want to die.

- It's too risky.
- I'm not crazy enough to do this.

Esther has just been asked to approach the king and ask for his help in overturning this decree; one that he signed and sealed with his signet ring and cannot be reversed. She is not a stupid queen. She realizes the huge risk that lies ahead of her. Is she willing to stand up to the king no matter the cost?

Mordecai comes back with some encouraging words (and maybe a little bit of fear) so Esther can see what great importance this is for the Jews. He gives the following reasons of why Esther should speak up for her people:

- Don't think that just because you live in the king's palace you will escape this. (Esther 4:13)
- If you keep silent, God is still going to work in the lives of the Jews and free them. However, you won't be the one He uses to do that. (Esther 4:14)
- Maybe you have come into royal dignity for such a time as this. (Esther 4:14)

I want to take a little closer look at the second reason Mordecai gives. It's one that I think is important for us to realize in understanding God and His plans. If God calls us to something and we say no or we give up and quit in the middle of it, God's divine purpose will still be accomplished on this earth with or without us.

But, who will have lost in this calling?

It will be us.

We will have missed out on something great for our lives. We will have missed out on being used by God. And we could potentially have missed out on the very sole purpose and reason for which we were created.

In the book called *Be Committed: Doing God's Will Whatever the Cost,* by Warren Weirsbe, he writes:

> *"Mordecai emphasized that God will accomplish His purposes even if His servants refuse to obey His will. If Esther rejected the will of God for her life, God could still save His people, but Esther would be the loser."*[11]

Esther could have missed out on being used by God for a really big purpose. If she had listened to her mind and believed all those excuses, then she would not have been used by God.

We know God has a big plan for each of us. When He calls us, He equips us (Hebrews 13:21). We aren't to be afraid of what He's called us to do. We aren't supposed to spout off excuses for not being able to accomplish this task. And we especially aren't supposed to give up and quit. God has called us to a particular task because He knows we can do it. Why? Because He has equipped us to do it.

---

11 Warren Wiersbe, *Be Committed*: Doing God's Will Whatever the Cost (Colorado Springs: David C. Cook, 1993), 126-127

Esther does not give in to those excuses. She does not listen to her mind, but instead listens to her heart. She ends up saving her people from death. She was willing to be used by God to accomplish His purpose on this earth.

### *Finding Freedom*

I'll be honest and admit to you that trying to overcome the fear I have of giving up when God calls is extremely hard. When God started working on my heart and all of my fears, He helped me to see that nothing is impossible for Him and He can break through any old habit or pattern in my life, including this fear of giving up.

How does one overcome this fear? I think we need to take another look at Esther. Her story points us in the right direction when it comes to showing us what steps a person should take when we feel like giving up.

### *Step One: Fast*

"Then Esther said in reply to Mordecai, 'Go, gather all the Jews to be found in Susa, and hold a fast on my behalf, and neither eat nor drink for three days, night or day. I and my maids will also fast as you do'" (Esther 4:15-16).

*Fasting? Really? You can't be serious.*

That's probably what you are saying to me right about now. And then you are listing off all the excuses as to why you could never fast. Now, I am not saying you have to be just like Esther and fast for three days and nights. But, what I am saying is that fasting is a spiritual practice that has helped others focus on God.

Warren Wiersbe says, *"Of itself, fasting is no guarantee that God will bless, for fasting must be accompanied by sincere humility and brokenness before the Lord."*[12] What he's saying basically is that our hearts have to be in the right place when we fast. We can't just decide that we need to fast in order to hear from the Lord and just do it because we feel like we're supposed to do it. We must be sincere about it and truly want to hear from the Lord.

How does one fast and what does that even look like? A fast could be from food. You may have done something like this during Lent. You give up a food you love and sacrifice it for the next forty days. When I've done that in the past, I find that I don't go back to that food. One year I gave up caffeinated sodas. That was fifteen years ago and I haven't had a caffeinated soda since then. I drank caffeine free sodas for a while after that, but eventually quit those all together, too.

Giving up a food during Lent is great, but the one thing we must remember is that it's not just about the sacrifice. It's about replacing that food with the Lord. We need not say we'll give up desserts for forty days and that be all. We need to truly be committed to spending time with the Lord and learning more about Him. It's about

---

12 Warren Wiersbe, *Be Committed: Doing God's Will Whatever the Cost* (Colorado Springs: David C. Cook, 1993) ,128

sacrificing what we love and replacing it with the Almighty Father…the one who longs for you to be with Him.

A fast can also be from things that are distracting you from the Lord. As I mentioned in chapter two, I fasted for twenty-one days. And my fast was from social media and TV. I can sure waste some time on my phone or iPad, scrolling through Facebook, Instagram, and Twitter. And then there's the joy of Netflix. It has the ability to turn me into a binge-watching monster. Who knew I could be sucked into social media and TV like that!

Was it easy? Not at all! It took all I had in me not to give in. But friends, I did it. I came out of it with a peace and a desire to continue to seek the Lord. I wrote a chapter in my book during those twenty-one days, which was a record for me. But, most importantly, that fast helped me find the Lord. His Word encouraged me to keep going and not let this fear triumph over me. I was not going to give up writing this book because someone out there needed to hear my story of fear and how Jesus has helped me through it.

Do you want to give up and are afraid you are close to doing it? Then fast. Give up something that you know is keeping you from continuing on this journey of God's calling. Seek the Lord during this fast. And I guarantee that you will find Him.

### Step Two: Pray

In Esther's story, God is not mentioned by name, but we can be sure that her actions come from God. When she asks everyone to fast with her, I am most certain she prays as well.

Warren Wiersbe says: *"Fasting and prayer are frequently found together in Scripture, for fasting is a preparation for concentrated and humble prayer."*[13] It's hard to fast and not pray. They go hand in hand. When you are seeking the Lord and fasting, you spend time in conversation with God. You talk with Him and share your heart with Him. Tell Him why you are afraid. Ask Him to show you what's holding you back and what's making you want to give up. I promise He will reveal those things to you.

Most importantly during this prayer time, make sure you listen as well. We can get so caught up in our talking that we forget to actually be still and listen. When you ask God to show you why you want to give up, you can't just stop there. You must actually listen. God will help you see the reasons why you want to give up on what He's calling you to do. It might be painful to hear, but when you cry out to God, He will be honest and show you why you give up easily.

In Daniel 9, Daniel is seeking an answer from God. So, what do you think Daniel did?

"Then I turned to the Lord God, to seek an answer by prayer and supplication with fasting and sackcloth and ashes" (Daniel 9:3).

---

13 Warren Wiersbe, *Be Committed: Doing God's Will Whatever the Cost* (Colorado Springs: David C. Cook, 1993) ,128

When Daniel needed to hear from God, he prayed and fasted. My friends, you need to do the same. I know it's hard, but we must learn from the examples of Esther and Daniel and take the time to fast and pray and seek the Lord.

### Step Three: Spend Time in the Word

Again, we do not see it mentioned in Esther that she opened her Bible and read God's Word. But, we know she fasted, prayed, and sought the Lord's guidance for this situation. For us, part of our hearing from God comes from His Holy Word, the Bible.

During my twenty-one day fast, I opened up the Scripture every day and read. I was hungry, thirsty and I had a strong desire to hear from God. I sought Him with all I had and that included opening up the God-breathed Word and finding Him there. God jumped out to me in every way possible. It was so cool to see how His Word helped me see Him and feel His peace on this fear I had of giving up on His calling, which was to write this book.

### Step Four: Live Your Faith Boldly

I love how boldly Esther lived her faith. She was willing to go to the extreme to do God's will and save the Jews, her people. The end of chapter 4 in verse 16 says:

"I will go to the king, though it is against the law; and if I perish, I perish" (Esther 4:16b).

Now that is pretty bold. She was willing to do all it takes to follow God, including dying. She was willing to follow Him no matter the cost. What if King Xerxes had been in a bad mood that day? What if he was appalled that a woman would come to him even when she wasn't called? She could have easily been killed that day. But, she wasn't. She didn't let her fear stop her. She didn't give up. She stayed committed to the calling that God had for her life. She had to be bold and live out her faith and do all she could to save her people.

God's calling in your life may be scary and terrifying to you. You might want to give up. But, I encourage you to live out your faith boldly. Don't stop because you hit a roadblock. Don't quit because you're overwhelmed. Don't give up because it's just too hard. Be bold. Live out your faith like Esther. Do all you can to persevere. Don't give up. Keep going.

The fear of giving up was real for me. It's a fear that I have every time I hear from the Lord. But, I have learned to conquer this fear by remembering what I learned from Esther. I was tired of living a life of being afraid of God's calling and just giving up. I wanted to be a woman who lived a life sold out for the Lord; a woman willing to do and go wherever God leads.

### Rise Up Prayer

*Giver of Life, You love us so much and desire for us to love You with our whole hearts. You long for a deep relationship with us, one where we will not fear but willingly go where You lead. But Lord, You also know there are many times where we give up too quickly or we give up without even thinking twice about it. We ask now for You to rise up, O Lord. Give us a faith that does not doubt, a confidence that does not shatter, and a heart that does not give up. Free us from the enemy who takes pleasure in watching us give up before we even really get a chance to live out Your calling for our lives. Lift up our eyes to see You when we desire to give up. Show us that You are the way, the truth, and the life. In Jesus' name, Amen.*

# IT'S TIME
## *Letting Go and Rising Up*

As I look back over this book, I am blown away by the almighty power of the Lord. The fears I have endured have buckled me at times. It has been difficult to stand up and serve the Lord because of these fears. Some days it was a struggle to even remember why God called me and why God wanted to use me.

Now I can see how powerful our God is. Every fear that was thrown my way by the enemy, God helped me overcome. I let fear consume me, but realizing I can find freedom in serving Him is truly amazing. Fear has no stronghold over me anymore. I am free.

My friends, it's time for you to call out to God and ask Him to rise up. Allow Him to cut you free from any fear that binds you and won't let you move. Let God be your Protector, your Defender, your Rock, your Sword, your

Shield, and your Deliverer. He is able to do anything. You just have to be willing to let Him.

We must realize that God goes before us in all we do, in our home life and in our work life. He never takes us to a place where He hasn't already walked. He won't misguide us or lead us astray. He will walk in front of us. He is our Shield who deflects all fears the enemy shoots at us.

We know God goes before us because of what He says in the Bible. There are many examples of this, but I want to focus on one that is powerful.

> "This is what the Lord says, 'I will go before you, Cyrus, and level the mountains. I will smash down gates of bronze and cut through bars of iron. And I will give you treasures hidden in the darkness-- secret riches. I will do this so you may know that I am the Lord, the God of Israel, the one who calls you by name'" (Isaiah 45:2-3, NLT).

For me, these verses are a perfect imagery of how God walks before us and takes away our fears. No matter what we face in life, whether it be personal or ministry-related, God goes before us. He walks before us and levels that mountain we believe is too high to climb. When we come to the gates we believe keep us from moving forward (which is fear in this case), He smashes it down and cuts through the bars of iron. Did you catch that? God is so powerful that He can knock over mountains and cut through bars of iron. There is nothing we will face that God cannot overcome.

I love the next verse that says that He will give us treasures hidden in the darkness, which are secret riches. During fearful times, those treasures for me have become Scripture verses. That's one reason why I decorate my house in Scripture. I want to be able to see God's Word. It helps me remember and focus on Him during those fearful times. Scripture provides me with comfort and peace. I am so thankful for God's Word.

Everyone tells me that once you hit your 40's the memory starts to fade a little. I believe that. I have found my memory is not as sharp as it used to be. I can't recall things like I used to. That realization sent a fearful moment into my life as I was reading the Bible one day. What if I forget God's Word? What if I can't remember Bible verses like I once could? What if, Lord?

That day God sent me the perfect Scripture verse to help calm my soul, it was my hidden treasure in the darkness… "I write to you young people, because you are strong and the word of God abides in you, and you have overcome the evil one" (1 John 2:14b).

God's Word abides in me. There is no need to fear forgetting what is written upon my heart…words I have recalled over the course of my life. God's Word will not fade because I am strong. I have overcome the evil one and fear will not overcome me.

What is your treasure that is hidden in the darkness? Perhaps it's Scripture like it is for me. Or maybe it's a person God uses to show you that fear is not powerful over you. Or maybe it's a song God gives to you at just the right moment. No matter what your treasure is, I pray you will look for it, even when you cannot see what lies ahead. Search for it and remember God goes before you. He has leveled the mountain. He has cut through the bars of iron. There is no need to fear what lies ahead of you....God goes before you.

Many times we have gone before the Lord. We have tried to rise up first before we ask God to rise up. We have tried to conquer our fears without the power of the Lord. I know that from personal experience. As you read throughout this book, you have seen the road of fear I have walked. You have read my story and seen that I have been a fearful person, especially when it comes to serving the Lord. I have been afraid of His call, of learning more about Him, of being lonely, of change, of criticism from others, of persons in authority, of not being good enough, of moving, of not being heard, of failing God, and of giving up. That is a lot of fear when it comes to serving the Lord. In each of these fears, I have tried to go before the Lord. I thought I could handle it, or even run away from the fear, hoping to avoid it and not face it.

And that's when I had it backwards.

I learned I should never try to do things on my own. I'm not strong enough. I am only strong when I walk with the Lord. In each chapter of this book I have shared with you how God showed me the path to finding freedom. And I learned this from His Holy Word. His Word is alive! It's not some ancient book (like some may think). It's a book that is God-breathed (2 Timothy 3:16) and it applies to our lives today. God speaks to us through it and it is powerful.

Even though I have overcome these fears in my life of serving the Lord, I know Satan will throw them back in my face…again, and again, and again. Satan doesn't use new tricks. He likes to use the same tools over and over. I know there will be days when I let the fear creep back in and keep me from stepping out and finding freedom, but I must remember how faithful God has been, how God has already defeated fear for me, how God has shown me the path to overcoming this fear in my life. And then I must rise up. God is the one who will protect me and the one who will light my path so I can clearly see Him.

God does the same for you, too, my friend. Let go of your fears. Be all who God created you to be. Stand firm on His promises. Be bold. Be courageous. Believe in His power and His love for you. Because when you do, you can boldly serve Him without fear.

It's time.

Rise up and serve the Lord.

# *Further Reading List*

I wanted to include some books that have encouraged me through this journey of overcoming fear. I hope you will check these out and find these helpful to you as well:

*Anxious for Nothing,* Max Lucado
*Goliath Must Fall,* Louie Giglio
*What Women Fear,* Angie Smith
*What Happens When Women Walk in Faith,* Lysa TerKeurst
*What Happens When Women Say Yes to God,* Lysa TerKeurst
*The Circle Maker,* Mark Batterson
*Audacious,* Beth Moore
*Fear Fighting,* Kelly Balarie

## *About the Author*

VANESSA MYERS is a graduate of Duke Divinity School and has been serving in the ministry for 17 years. She is the Children's Director at Dahlonega United Methodist Church in Dahlonega, GA. She is married to Andrew and they have two children. She enjoys sharing about her faith, family, and ministry on her blog: *www.vanessamyers.org*.

CPSIA information can be obtained
at www.ICGtesting.com
Printed in the USA
LVHW09s0032060918
589319LV00006B/94/P